MY WHITSTABLE 1920 - 1939

by

Jean Skinner

*This book is dedicated
to my family especially
Matthew, Hannah and David.*

June 1998

Copyright © Jean Skinner 1998

All rights reserved. No part of this publication may be reproduced, stored in a retrieval system or transmitted in any form or by any means electronic, photocopying, recording or otherwise; without the prior permission of the Copyright holder.

ISBN: 1 899177 05 1

Typeset and printed in Great Britain by

Oyster Press (Whitstable)
110 John Wilson Business Park
Chestfield
Whitstable
Kent
CT5 3QT

Telephone: (01227) 772605 Fax: (01227) 772606

Published by Oyster Press (Whitstable) Kent

First Edition

Photograph on page 55 from the Valentine Collection courtesy of the St Andrews University Library

MY WHITSTABLE 1920-1939

Contents

	Page
Introduction	2-3
Poem	2
Acknowledgements	3
Section One - My memories of Whitstable 1920-1939	5-57
Chapter One - Walkabout	5-22
Chapter Two - The Twenties	23-32
Chapter Three - The Thirties	33-39
Chapter Four - The Seasons	40-51
Chapter Five - Things I remember	52-55
Chapter Six - Snippets from 'The Whitstable Times'	56-57
Section Two - Whitstable (specific)	**59-120**
Chapter Seven - Wartime	59-62
Poem - A Place for Them	59
War Casualties 1914-1918	60-61
War Casualties 1939-1945	61-62
Chapter Eight - Whitstable People	63-83
Celebrities	63-73
Notorious Whitstable	73-75
Some Well-Known Residents	76-83

			Page
Chapter Nine -	Education		84-88
Chapter Ten -	Victoria Street		89
	Streets and Occupants 1920, 1930, 1939		90-120

Section Three — **Life between the Wars** — **121-133**

Chapter Eleven	-	Comparisons and Memories	121-124
		Cost of food and other items	125-127
		Cigarettes and tobacco	127-128
		Newspapers, journals, etc	129-131
		Services	132-133

Section Four — **And finally ....** — **135-137**

Chapter Twelve	-	Final Thoughts	135-137
	-	Notes	138

We met, we married, a long time ago.

He worked long hours, and wages were low.

No telly, no radio, no bath, times were hard.

A cold water tap, toilet in yard,

No holidays abroad, no carpets on floors.

We'd coal on the fire, we never locked doors.

Our children arrived, no pill in those days,

And brought them up without state aid.

No Valium, no drugs, no LSD.

We cured our pains with a good cup of tea.

Were you sick, you was treated at once,

Not fill in a form and come back next month.

No vandals, no muggings, there was nought to rob.

You were rich with a couple of bob.

Milkmen and paper boys would whistle and sing.

A night at the flicks, a wonderful thing.

We had our share of trouble and strife

But had to face it, that was life.

Now I look back through the years

I remember the blessings, not the tears.

Acknowledgements

When I embarked on writing this book about Whitstable and the life of the average working class family between the wars, I imagined it would be very simple just jotting down my memories and elaborating on them. This was not the case - for every subject there is research to be done and this has not been easy as records have not been kept locally. Also, with changes that have taken place such as the introduction of the Health Service in 1948, and the nationalisation and privatisation of public service, records have either been mislaid or vanished during the reorganisation. This has been a great challenge although at times I have felt like tearing my hair out, not knowing where to go or who to ask to answer my questions. However, I've learned many things whilst doing this. It could not have been achieved without the co-operation of old friends and folk that I have met during the last three years. To these I say very sincerely "Many Thanks":

Joan and Les Rogers; Grace Catling; Wanda Morgan; Charlie Chester; Mr and Mrs Aubrey Pearce; Betty Innes Smith; Fred Pursey; Walter Fisher; Mrs Fisk; Mrs Forster; Gordon Knowles; Stan Hadler; Mr G Surman; Mr Gaywood; Mr W Court; Jim Laker; R Childs; Jack Daniels; St Alphege Church.

I also thank the following organisations for their invaluable help in getting information from their archives:

Law Society; Bank of England; British Telecom; Post Office; Canterbury Cathedral and Museum; Gas Board; British and Whitstable Libraries; Social Security; The Whitstable Times.

Many thanks to Oyster Press for their help.

Last, but certainly not least, to my family, who have listened to and tolerated my moaning when I felt frustrated in not finding the answers to my many queries and to my daughter, Sally, for preparing this epistle to present to the publishers.

SECTION ONE

My memories of Whitstable
1920-1939

Chapter One

WALKABOUT

I left my home town, Whitstable, on 3 September 1939 at nineteen years of age to work and live in Highbury, North London. I have been back many times to see relations and friends and to stay with my sister in nearby Herne Bay, and had lived there again for a short period in the late 1940s. A few years ago, on one of my visits, I began to think back to what life had been like in this small seaside town between the wars - the time when I was a child and young woman.

I hadn't realised how much it had changed until I compared it with my schoolfriends' memories and so I decided to walk along the streets that I knew so well and note in detail the changes that had inevitably taken place.

I decided to start my pilgrimage from the harbour gates, noted the improvement at Starvation Point and remembered in the 1920s Gann and Brown, coal office, Stretelys Dining Rooms, H K Daniels' offices where men waited outside, presumably for a berth on one of his barges or on any ship that came into the harbour, and the Railway Tavern (no longer there). This little corner was a very busy part of the town but, as time passed into the 1930s, it became an eyesore with the buildings run down, empty and depressing. No wonder it was named Starvation Point. I found walking along the Sea Wall depressing - gone were the craftsmen who occupied the small lock-up workshops: Mr Ward, the shoe repairer; Goldfinches, the sailmakers who made the dark red heavy canvas sails for the barges and small sails for yachts but no longer hearing the old treadle sewing machine; Mr Leney, the blacksmith, who made parts for boats and yachts as well as horse-shoeing and the wonderful wrought iron work for which he was awarded the bronze medal at the Kent Agricultural Show. It was wonderful to watch him create a work of art from a crude bar of iron - gone was the tap tap tapping of the hammer against the anvil. Talking to him was a one-sided affair for he was as deaf as a post. The forge no longer exists as such - now there's only a dilapidated storeroom. Further along Mr Parsons kept his wicker barrow - not in a shed, more a hole in the wall. This vehicle was for delivering parcels for Carter Paterson who also had a depot at the bottom of Victoria Street and for the Post Office at Christmas time. Along to Reeves Beach - how sad that the sea wall had to be built. Very necessary but it does nothing to enhance the appearance.

Apparently, in the early 1920s, the yacht park was a skating rink. I don't remember this but I do recall the tea rooms above.

I was intrigued to see a green house on the rear of the house next to Stone House - very cheerful and providing a spot of colour - and so along to the Horsebridge, passing Sheppey View, at one time the Stag Public House, and houses whose appearances have changed for the better.

I called in at the Pearsons Arms and was taken aback by the transformation. It's now a chic restaurant and inn specialising in seafood cuisine with a totally different clientele from that served by Beryl Waters and her father, but the atmosphere of the pub of pre-war days has gone. Then it was frequented by fishermen, oyster dredgers, shipyard workers and men from the coalyards. Beryl was a very jovial person who always had an answer to the men's banter - she was 'one of the boys'.

Sitting on the sea wall, I was conscious how quiet it was and thought back to the activity there used to be from the harbour gates to the Horsebridge and remembering the oyster fisheries and the thousands and thousands of barrels of oysters that had passed through those doors to grace the tables of many famous hotels and restaurants all over the world. Generations of local men had worked there since 1793. No activity from Anderson Perkins and

Rigdens as the shipyards were closed in the 1930s and the slipway made redundant.

Looking towards the harbour, I noticed the lighthouse had vanished and barges were no longer coming round the head, their huge red sails in full splendour. The majority relied on sails and there was only one to my knowledge that boasted an engine, *The Kathleen*. The barges were such a feature of the North Kent coast and a few working examples have survived, as shown below:

Name	Master	Where they are now
SAVOY	G Fryer	Houseboat
HKD (ex JEWISH)	C Hubbard E Eldrick A Fryer	Loss by mine 1941
LORD CHURCHILL	J Olive	Believed sunk
AZIMA	B Fryer	Used as a jetty at Otterham
TRILBY	E Payton	There were two
DULUTH	A Fryer	Hit sunken wreck bank 1941
GLOBE	V Rowden N Laker	Loss by mine February 1941 Two crew lost
THOMAS and FRANCIS	C Merritt	Derelict by 1947
WHY NOT	? Lissenden	Sunk in collision 1932
W H RANDALL	E Kemp	Broken up approximately 1928
COSBY SALLY	? Shrubsole	Broken up
VICUNIA	A Kelsey	Unknown
KATHLEEN	F Wraight Snr and Jr	Houseboat under refurbishment

Name	Master	Where they are now
CEREAL	V Rowden	Capsized
DORAN	E Kemp	Unknown
CAMBRIA	B Roberts	Maritime Trust Greenwich 1970
ONWARD	M Walters	Broken up
ARDWINA	B Fryer	Unknown
PAGALSHAM	?	Unknown
NORTH DOWN	? Jemmet	Houseboat last seen Cubitts Wharf 1992
JAMES and HARRIET	? Shrubsole	Sunk off The Sportsman
SYBIL	?	Unknown

Cremers of Faversham

Name	Master	Where they are now
ESTHER	P Whitish	For sale 1984
ETHEL (renamed Pride of Sheppey)	T Massey	Sunk off Sheerness
PRETORIA	C Frate / D Whitish	Broken up
DECIMA	D Whitish	Houseboat
JANE and ANN	A Keam	Houseboat believed in Cornwall

I have tried to find data to complete this list but have been unable to do so. According to records, Cremers barges discharged the cargo of sawn timber off the Horsebridge to be loaded onto horse-drawn carts.

Looking over to Sheppey, the skyline has changed. On a clear day, high rise buildings - presumably in Essex - can be seen. At Leysdown on Sheppey, a large area is now a caravan site where before it appeared green.

There is no longer an oyster fleet, only one oyster smack, *The Gamecock*, which is there to remind us of our once famous industry. No Cremers barges, anchored off the Horsebridge and bringing in wood, and horses and carts carrying it inshore.

The turrets way out in the sea were erected during the war to alert the authorities of air raids and a possible invasion and of attack bombers on their way to London. After the war, one was occupied by 'Screaming' Lord Sutch for a pirate radio station. After he left, he formed the joke political party, The Monster Raving Loony Party.

Leaving the Horsebridge, I felt very sad to think that this part of the town is now devoid of the industries that for generations had been the mainstay of Whitstable.

So along to Island Wall. The houses, once shabby, were very much improved, looking smart and cared for. The two general shops and the Guinea Inn are now private houses with the fish and chip shop - renowned for its potato fritters - now replaced by smart council flats extending round to Waterloo Road. A few houses have been demolished for a day centre. Apart from Mrs Dadds' little front room shop, which is again a private house, it has remained the same. Back to Island Wall, passing Anderson Perkins and Rigdens, the now vacant shipyard and the People's Free Mission whose pastor, Mr Skinner (no relation), owned the gentlemen's outfitters in the High Street. At one time, inquests were held there. *The Favourite*, an oyster yawl, has been restored (almost) to its former glory and now has a permanent home between two houses, 'Starboard Lights' and 'The Favourite'. Along to the Neptune and passing the spot where the training ships of the Sea Cadets stood.

What has happened to the Red Spider cafe and the Boating Lake?

Coming back to the Golf Cottages, where Wanda Morgan and the acting family, the Liveseys, resided and noting that new houses have been built at the rear of West Beach houses and so to Nelson Road, passing Stevens' General Shop. Apart from Kennetts greengrocers and Petts Dairy, which is now a private house, it has remained the same across the Salts where fairs, circuses and other events took place and to the estate built by Stanley Reeves, Mr Saunders' school, now a private house, through to Middle Wall, passing the Congregational Hall, now the United Reform Church. Opposite there used to be the primary Sunday School which is now the entrance to the dressing rooms of the Playhouse Theatre, at one time the Congregational Church.

Mrs Barratt's Hand Laundry is now a private house. Until the war, Middle Wall was considered a slum area for in the late twenties the council started a clearance scheme and a number of houses were demolished. Everything that could be was burned and the occupants were rehoused on a new estate at the lower part of Station Road and Westmeads Road. To those folks, it must have been heaven to live in a modern house with electricity and a bathroom and with the fear of floods gone. I have been told that the rent was 8/6d per week - today this seems incredible. Those houses that were left have been modernised and there is now a car park where the others stood.

The two public houses, the *Smack* and the *Wall Tavern*, have been refurbished. Mr Moyes' shoe repair shop has disappeared, the Post Office in the High Street has moved to Gladstone Road and the sorting office to Cromwell Road. There are no longer telegraph boys on their cycles or postmen with vans and handcarts coming in and out of the sorting office at the rear of the post office.

The Baptist Church remains, Rigden's vegetable shop is a private house, the PDSA hut that treated sick animals free of charge is no longer there and the sea cadets have their headquarters in Bonners Alley.

Houses by Meads Alley that were damaged by enemy action have been replaced by modern houses. Down Terrys Lane to the High Street where the East Kent garage and booking office stood. These were destroyed by enemy action and there is now an open air fruit market and a large indoor market. Passing the Assembly Hall and where Mr Amos had his photographic studio and a cafe damaged in the same incident to the building first occupied by the Fire Brigade, then the Ambulance Station - now vacant - to the Council Baths and Toilets. Baths were 2d and very popular as few people had bathrooms. These are now just toilets. Crossing over to Sea Street - Browning coalyard has gone, the Prince of Wales public house is now Alberres restaurant (very chic) and Snobby Hopkins in Red Lion Lane has gone. Before coming to Leggetts Lane, there were two houses, one occupied by the Foad family. One of their children was killed by a car and shortly after this tragic accident and as more cars appeared, Sea Street became one-way. Matthews and Tritton's garage next door and Porters building yard are no longer there so it's back to the harbour which, for many years, was so very very busy. I notice that at the entrance there is now a very much-needed lifeboat and the Customs and Excise building and where the Steam Packet stood is now the Whitstable Rowing Club. I remember the Steam Packet surrounded by laurel bushes with an entrance at either side to the harbour. Mr Wills' cottage has disappeared. On the opposite side of the road, the reservoir - also known as the backwater - had gates which regulated the flow of water from the harbour. Now it has been covered over and is used as a car park, a weekly market and has kept the houses in Westgate Terrace and adjoining roads from flooding.

No longer are there railway lines, a level crossing, signal box nor booking office. Instead, there is a health centre and housing estate and, on the harbour side, a very narrow path and a high black fence behind which there were huts, sheds, nets and so on. This is now a garage and bowling alley. Until the early thirties, apart from the beaches and slopes, Tankerton wasn't considered a part of Whitstable - it gradually became built up.

Retracing my steps, I decided to walk along the streets leading from

Harbour Street and west along the alleyways at the back of Marmion Terrace past Mr Shilling's house where, as a child, I bought his home-cured bloaters. Everyone bought Shilling's bloaters. He used an upturned wooden box with the herrings hanging on a rod above smouldering sawdust. This home industry no longer exists. Into Bexley Street where Mr Sholl's boot repair shop no longer stands. Here, you could buy remnants of leather for a few pence. Along to Mr Sawyer's bakehouse and shop where you could buy fresh bread on a Sunday afternoon, passing through stable-type doors or, if you called early in the morning, 2d would buy a very large bag of yesterday's cakes. Passing the Police Station and Mr Johnson's grocery shop which is now vacant.

Do you remember the Scottish family that had its Waverley fish and chip shop (now a takeaway) where, whilst waiting to be served, you were given a pile of white paper about six inches square that lined the newspaper wrapping to rub with the first joint of your thumb to form a fan-shaped pile so that it was easier to pick up? The reward for this was a bag of crackling.

Walking up Harbour Place and passing a building on the left-hand side on the corner of St Peter's Road where Tolputts the rag and bone merchant stabled his horse, Trixey - this is now a garage. Opposite, Albion House, a large neglected building, is now flats - a great improvement. Further along, Burtons, the greengrocers, is now Finnerleys general shop, one of the few remaining small shops.

Along to Cromwell Road to Dobbies general shop that is now a bricked space with a seat. Until the mid-twenties, you had to walk along the side of a dyke to reach Sydenham Street via Acton Road. In the early thirties, the dyke from Acton Road to Church Road was covered and named Stream Walk.

Along Sydenham Street, remember Mr Fogg, the insurance agent? Money was taken to him, he did not collect it. Queues formed outside his house on the night the money was due and he had an awful parrot that was so spiteful and noisy.

St Peter's Church services were originally held at a Mission Hall in Bexley Street, at first a corrugated iron building, but in 1925 the present church was built and the iron building became the Scouts Hall in Acton Road.

Mr Beales, shoe repairer, Spilletts opposite and Harmans greengrocery shops are now private houses, Tilleys grocery shop on the corner of Bexley Street. Mr Tilley was a very jovial man - always wore a bowler hat - and sat in the cash desk at the weekend. When you paid your bill, you received a bar of chocolate. If your goods were delivered, you found a bar of chocolate among the groceries. This was a real old-fashioned grocery shop. When you entered the shop, you passed stacks of tins of loose biscuits and the top layers had glass lids. You moved on to the mahogany counter on which stood large brass scales and stacks of tinned fruit and vegetables on either side, large metal containers holding pulses such as lentils, pearl barley, etc and the shelves stacked with merchandise at the rear. The provision counter held large blocks of butter and margarine to be patted into half pound and one pound slabs with wooden pats; a selection of large rounds of cheese to be cut to the required amount by a cheese wire, bladders of lard which are not seen today, sides of bacon hanging all exposed, sacks of coconut and sugar on the floor - this would not be allowed today. I nearly forgot the large box of broken biscuits. Very few items came in prepacked. The main suppliers of prepacked tea were Lyons, Brooke Bond and Mazawatte. Another feature of stores such as Tilleys was the well-dressed window display. This shop, like so many small shops, no longer trades. This is now a bricked up area.

Along to Albert Street. Coleman's coalyard, the Primitive Methodist Church dilapidated, Mrs Smith's haberdashery and dress shop and Warners general shop now private houses. Mrs Warner was a religious woman who quoted the Bible to children when she felt they needed it. Mrs Church's shop where, if you took a basin, you could purchase 1d worth of Golden Syrup or pickles and, on the week before Boat Race day, they sold emblems displaying the colours of the two teams for $\frac{1}{2}$d. This is now a hairdressers. Mrs Appleton's opposite also had a coal shed at the rear and children used to take their handmade carts for maybe seven or 14 lbs of coal. Her speciality was homemade toffee apples and I haven't tasted their equal since - they were superb. On reflection, I wonder if coal dust was an added ingredient. Who cares? Warners, Smiths and Appletons are now private houses. Mrs Butcher's shop is still open and is run by her daughter. I was disappointed at not being greeted by a loud clanging bell but by a much quieter one. I associate this shop with Nelsons gelatine gums - by returning the 10 discs from these you received a football.

Crossing St Peter's Street, I noticed the Cookery School and the Foresters Arms and the Fountain Inn in Sydenham Street are unoccupied.

As a child I remember my grandmother sending me along the alleys with a jug to buy 2d of stout. Do you remember Mr Philpot and Mr Foad who owned greyhounds and trained them in the Recreation Ground and Mr Horne's newspapers which he sold from his front room?

At the top of Albert Street, John Kemps builders yard is now a studio. The little adjacent cottage has gone as has Mr Foad's garage. There is now a car park leading through to Victoria Street and I noticed that the original door of the Palais is still there. Opposite the slaughter house at the rear of Allen's butchers shop is now closed. This is where, as children, we watched the squealing pigs being taken down the cobbled passages to be slaughtered and the ice cart carrying large blocks of ice as fridges - a thing of the future - were not yet installed.

Nuttens coal office is now a bridal boutique and their stables have gone as has the small cottage. Mr Lockyers upholstery shop, later Mr Bolton's fishing tackle shop, Mr Tilley's house at the rear of the stables which housed my grandfather's (Merritt) horses and carriages, and opposite the two houses have gone as has No 6A which, in the twenties, was Mr West's antique shop and dolls' hospital and later became Mr Foreman's antique shop. No 6 was Mrs Ashby's greengrocery shop and Mr Blyth's house which displayed a sign which you would not see today - "Window Cleaner and Carpet Beater".

Then I was at a loss.

What a terrifying night 11 October 1941 must have been when you consider the number of houses that was demolished in such a thickly populated area. Mercifully there were few casualties thanks to the Morrison shelters.

Houses Nos 7 - 17 have been replaced by new houses. Crossing Bexley Street, houses Nos 19 - 39, including Mr Savage's shop, are now Victoria Flats. Opposite Nos 10 - 34 there is a car park. Squibber Camburn's house, where a haircut, shingled or bobbed and singed, cost 6d and a gentlemen's barber and Mrs Dowley's general shop are now private houses.

The remainder of Victoria Street has remained the same, except that Carter Paterson's office has gone.

I cannot leave Victoria Street without mentioning Mrs Weller. Do you remember her at No 61? A tall, rotund lady who was renowned for her homemade toffees, treacle, creamy coconut and fig and nut brittle displayed on a round table covered with a snow white lace tablecloth. The sweets were weighed on a small pair of scales to the exact amount of 2d a quarter.

Now to Warwick Road, looking to the right. The only difference are the new houses where Mr Usher had his diary demolished by enemy action. Opposite, the general shop is now a Spar store. Going back to the bottom of Albert Street where Stanley Reeves builders yard stood until 1932, the first victim of the arsonist who also fired the home of the Gifford family.

Through to Westgate Terrace, Nurse Walters' nursing home and Keillers greengrocery shop are now private houses, along Reservoir Road to Diamond Road. I was very surprised to see that Bambrick's Model Laundry had closed after so many years and the pen nib factory which was opened in 1929 is also closed. The houses destroyed by enemy action have been rebuilt. Through to Cromwell Road where Johnson's sweet shop is again a private house, Smith's the builder's house is now replaced by newly-built houses, Seaths timber yard, another victim of the arsonist, is now the post office and sorting office. Haywards coach builders is now the Whistable Times office. Next to the Church hall is a vets on the spare piece of ground and No 164, Marine Equipment, and at the entrance to the Recreation Ground was a large hut occupied by a wonderful organisation, Age Concern, which runs a day centre for the elderly there and which has now moved to Vulcan Avenue.

Looking at the recreation ground, I remember the fun we had having grass fights after the mowers had been busy, the picnics and kite flying. I had an Atlanta kite but it was commandeered by my father who competed against other fathers who had done the same thing to their children. They battled to see whose kite flew the highest or did the most tricks. In the early 30s, swings and seesaws arrived and shows such as the Fur and Feather were held. Apparently, in 1923, the Council bought the five acres. The piece of ground adjoining the Drill Hall was used by the Sea Cadets and later by Foads as a garage. The Drill Hall was, and I believe still is, the home of the 1st 4th Battalion of the Buffs and in the 30s the then Drum and Fife Band could be heard practising. At Christmas time it was a depot for parcels and as far back as 1923 dances were held there with music supplied by the Royal Native Jazz Band.

Along to the DIY shop, at one time allotments on which stood an enormous wooden hoarding on which were written excerpts from the Bible such as "The Wages of Sin is Death" and "The Gift of God is Eternal Life". It may be a part of the history but I was glad it was removed. Before becoming a DIY shop, it was formerly Weatherlys the bakers, opposite Hewetts shop which has reverted to a private house. May's dairy on the corner of Regent Street, later Reed's Dairy. Rowden's general shop on the corner of Acton Road, Steward's butchers shop, Osborne's general shop on the corner of St Peter's Street are all now private houses. Otherwise, along to St Peter's Street it has remained the same.

Argyle Road has not changed.

Apart from Camburn's Hand Laundry closing and the houses which have been built on the allotments leading to Skinner's Alley, King Edward Street has not changed. Theobald's slaughterhouse in Skinner's Alley is a private house. Do you remember that awful Carrion Crow that attacked people, especially cyclists?

Beresford Road is still unmade. Mr Laraman the market gardeners house is now business premises.

Gamble and Gisby's plumbers, Oldfield's forge and Frend's chicken farm are now different businesses.

In Hamilton Road, until 1926 a field, the Council built houses Nos 2 - 24 and private houses were built later in 1927.

Luffs sawmills is now Harcross's.

Mr White's general shop and Mrs Cage's house have gone. The building that was Conservative HQ and later the Auction Rooms was burned down. In 1933, Colonel Carnegie was responsible for the erection of the temporary building of the Hamilton Road Mission with the Sunday School at the rear.

Walking along Stream Walk, crossing Cromwell Road under the railway bridge where children practised acrobatics on the handrails, passing the passage opened up in the late 20s to the station and Dawkings and the station field which is now a housing estate, turning left to the station which has not changed except for the closure of Newling's shop opposite Douglas Avenue and houses being built on the wasteland next to the shop. Thurston Park opposite was once privately-owned, a private estate since 1937.

London's Field opposite the station is now shops and an estate with roads leading to the Ivy House estate. Then, along to the railway bridge. I said the railway bridge - where has it gone with everything associated with it? That's another item of local history which has vanished. This railway bridge was thought to be the oldest in the world but it was, in fact, the second eldest, the first being at Bogshole. This was forgotten until recently. The demolition of the Church Street bridge is unforgivable, nothing less than sheer vandalism with not as much as a plaque to mark where it stood. Words cannot express what I and many more think of this despicable and outrageous act. If it were too low or too narrow, traffic could have been diverted via Teynham Road. If it needed repairing, I am sure that if an appeal had been launched the cash would have been forthcoming. Now this is just another road where before it had been unique and historical.

So to Scammels Corner, named after the original owner of the garage and general shop, later Crosslands garage and Ken Hayward's shop. A post office was installed in 1936 but the shop has since been demolished.

Opposite there were fields parallel with the railway line and the backs of houses in Church Street, through to Ham Shades Lane, now a private estate. Also there is a new footbridge. Going towards Bartletts Corner, passing the Ivy House estate, built in the grounds of Ivy House which was once owned by the Andrews family to the All Saints Hall, built in 1939 for the enormous sum of £3500 on the site of the "Olde Forge", later a shop for Kirbys furniture until it collapsed in 1930, next to the Monument Inn, that lovely olde worlde cottage, Meadowlands, where Miss Lamb had her kindergarten. Separating Meadowlands from Sommerville, Bertie Vidler had a market garden but he was unfortunately killed by a car opposite Haywards shop. His widow was awarded £915. One man who had had too much to drink passed the greenhouses and swore he saw Bertie standing in one of them. He sounded so convincing that people living in the Church Street area were very reluctant to go out at night.

Sommerville was the home of the Platt family who allowed the field adjoining the house to be used by churches to hold their summer treats. This is now a private housing estate. Passing Bartlett Corner, where Bartlett and Bissons prize herd of Jersey cows could be seen grazing. They boasted that the herd was TB tested which was quite something as TB was a killer disease and great concern was shown particularly where young schoolchildren were involved. A bomb destroyed a house here. Luckily, no one was killed. Crossing over the Thanet Way to South Street, there are more houses to the South Street level crossing but no rails or station. Carrying on to Radfall, I then turned back to Herne Bay Road. Again there are new housing estates to Clovers Rise and here I was completely lost. When I left in 1939 there were a few houses, lots of fields and unmade roads to Chestfield. These fields were used by families during holiday time for picnics. I remember in the late 20s a lorry carrying scouts (not local) passing over the small bridge and capsizing, killing a few of the boys.

So back to Herne Bay Road to Ham Shades Lane and the hospital. When the hospital was built in 1926 it was surrounded by fields where my father took me to pick blackberries and I remember the hedges of wild roses. Coming back along Queen's Road, I thought of the number of times I had cycled along that road collecting and delivering grocery orders and back to the station via Teynham Road. Until 1932 there was no bridge. Teynham Road finished where the bridge has now been built. Through to Railway Avenue, to the station. The forecourt has much improved but the station, once so busy and the booking office with the newspaper kiosk and taxis parked outside is now closed, looking very sad and neglected. I then decided to stand on the footbridge to see if I could recapture the thrill and excitement watching the train coming around the bend, filling the bridge with steam. Alas, no. Those magnificent giants have now been replaced with the impersonal diesel trains, and the romance of the railways has gone forever. Turning right from the station along to Church Road, the allotments just past Stream Walk are now a general shop. Pass the Belmont Ground where so many events were held and which is now homes and the Football and Cricket Club. Passing what used to be the Gas and Light Company's yard and furnaces until 1930 when the gas was diverted from Dover, but remained for a while as the office and maintenance yard. No more coal and coke is delivered from the yard, the small shop has gone and there is now a highrise block of flats. Amos and Foads building yard has gone, Mrs Putwain's dressmaking room and Mr Putwain's shoe repair shop have gone and the Railway Inn has closed.

Going along Canterbury Road towards the Tollgate, there have been many changes. Haywards cycle shop closed after trading for 70 years. Charlie Knowles' house, "Jaffa", formerly Dunelm College, is now a block of flats. Dawkins Bakery is now a cafe and Granary House a home for the elderly. The forge was the scene of an horrendous murder in the late 20s.

In Grimshill Road, the bakery is now an insurance consultancy and the laundry is a gospel hall. Again, going towards Millstrood, houses are being built and a large block of council warden flats where there were allotments and fields. Roads from Grimshill Road led to a very large housing estate, council and private. In Essex Road, there are a few changes. Brownings stables are now the offices of Stroud and Roberts, Mr London's Star Mineral Company is now B D Motors and also St James' Court flats. In Harwich Street, Godfreys greenhouses have vanished and further along where Mr Alce had his carpentry business there are a number of small inlets.

Suffolk Street, Norfolk Street and Kent Street have remained very much the same.

I was disappointed that Glebe Way was very overgrown. Perhaps I saw it at the wrong time of the year.

Joy Lane appears very much the same except that Dawkins chocolate factory has gone as has the Shaftesbury Boys' Home which is now a very tasteful private estate. Going towards the Blue Anchor again where there were marshes there is now a council estate with shops and more private houses are being built in the various adjoining roads. There is also a very large caravan site.

Back to Borstal Hill. Carter's market garden and Mason's garage have been replaced by the fire station. The wide expanse of fields from Mr Coombs house to the windmill have been built on.

The mill and house were once owned by the Irving family, descendants of Sir Henry Irving, the famous Shakespearean actor. The last inhabitant was Lawrence Irving, the author and choreographer, who used the mill as his studio and then sold it to become a restaurant and motel. I understand that it has reverted to a private residence. The fields by the mill have been built upon. So many fields have been built upon. The Thanet Way, built about 1934, has cut through so much land separating Whitstable from so many villages. It was a great joy to walk across fields to the village without having to cope with a constant flow of traffic. Has the Thanet Way been an advantage to Whitstable, I wonder, for now it is bypassed?

So much for Whitstable.

Tankerton in the 20s grew from an expanse of fields to a thriving small town in the 30s. There were few private houses and various organisations had holiday homes. The Marine Hotel, which during the war was a hospital, and the Tankerton Hotel and George Fitts Motors growing from a tin shed repairing cycles and motor cycles to a flourishing garage. The hospital was completed in 1926. At that time, Whitstable folk visited Tankerton to take walks or visit the Lawn Pavilion or to go to the beaches and amusements which were very popular. Gradually roads were made and shops and houses appeared. The Tankerton Pavilion was built in 1930. The Towers were opened to the public in 1937. Visitors came and occupied flats and many of the residents were commuters to London.

Swalecliffe, again, was mostly fields. The Plough and The Wheatsheaf are not the original buildings. The old inns were situated at the road's edge. The Flying Circus was a very popular event before the war but no longer visits the field behind The Plough. Estates and shops were built. Swalecliffe Church and the coastguard cottages looked very isolated and lonely and are now surrounded by an estate with a caravan site nearby. In 1928 Chestfield Halt was built. Chestfield has not expanded quite so rapidly although more houses have been built and the approaches to the Barn from the Thanet Way have certainly been built upon.

One event I have forgotten to mention is the demolition of the Swalecliffe brickworks chimneys. I believe it was 1934 when they were scheduled to be demolished on a Sunday morning. This did not happen at the given time and people arriving to watch the operation from Tankerton Slopes found them already gone. Apparently it had taken more than one attempt to demolish them and there have been a number of versions of which method was used to bring them down.

For a number of years the sea has been claiming land on our coast. For instance, it was possible to walk from Whitstable to Herne Bay along the sea shore.

I cannot think of anything more to say that might interest you of the changes that have occurred along the highways and byways of my home town.

Chapter Two

THE TWENTIES

To divide history into decades is difficult for life goes on very much the same year after year particularly in a small seaside town devoid of industry which depends so much on activities associated with the sea for its survival.

After a war as traumatic as the 1914-1918 conflict, there were few homes - no matter the social status (and we were very conscious of this) - that were unaffected by husbands or sons having been killed (200) or disabled. Not only were the servicemen unsettled but also the womenfolk were finding it hard to adjust to normal family life again. This was a daunting task as there was very little help from the State for the widows and dependants.

To obtain Parish relief, there was a rigid means test. Apparently a scheme was launched enabling men to emigrate with government aid and some took advantage of this.

As a young child, you are not aware of the trials and tribulations of the parents. I do not remember this but have been told by folk in their eighties that it was not uncommon to see children attending school barefoot and to see the queues at the soup kitchens - how they scoff when they hear this time referred to as the GOOD OLD DAYS.

I suppose that, when you look at the lack of freedom today such as not allowing children out of their own, having to lock doors, fasten windows, not venturing out alone after dark, they were, but on the other side of the coin we have so much to be thankful for in so many ways.

As you get older, you realise how narrow the outlook on life was, probably through the lack of opportunity to travel. A day in Canterbury, a trip along the coast was something of an event.

Possibly a stay with relations. To have a week's holiday at a boarding house or hotel was unheard of and for many their holiday was working in the hop fields.

Superstitions were strongly believed. These old wives' tales usually applied to pregnancy. For example, if a woman was frightened by, say, a cat and touched her arm at the same time, the child would be born with a birthmark the shape of a cat on the arm. I don't know if my mother was frightened by a map of the British Isles as I have a small replica on the back of my hand!

Standards were different from today. If a woman had a child out of wedlock, it was a stigma that both mother and child carried for many a year. This was not so for the father. Maybe it was an age of virgin conceptions.

To "live in sin" was the cardinal sin with the woman sent to Coventry and people saying she should be ashamed of herself as well as that ridiculous saying, "She's no better than she should be", whatever that means. I'm sure I don't know. Again, very little was said of the man involved. If a woman entered a pub alone, she was only there for one reason!

The majority of marriages were between local people.

The man was the dominant figure in the household. What he said was law and the family was expected to adhere to his beliefs. It was the duty of the females to do the household chores as it was not considered a man's job to do so.

I am generalising, of course, as there were exceptions. To be fair, allotments had to be tended and shoes had to be mended from scraps of leather bought from the shoe repairers, Blakey's as well as hobnails to fix run down heels, rubber soles stuck on and round rubber heels fixed with a screw in the centre. Of an evening a visit to the local. Also it was not unusual to see groups of men standing around on street corners putting the world to rights. Outings were organised by the pub landlords and employers for men only.

For women, their sole job being that of housewife, few took outside employment. Those who did took on domestic work for others, such as washing or dressmaking.

I must mention that it was considered unwise for women to walk around the harbour area at night when visiting sailors were around as some were known to have been accosted and, as the story goes, hi-jacked for the white slave traffic.

As I have mentioned before, there was freedom of movement for children to play in the fields, woods and on the seashore, to walk along the railway banks, to play in the streets even after dark such games as hoops, hopscotch, flicking cigarette cards against the wall, skipping with the rope tied to lamp posts. There were few cars.

I mentioned the freedom children had but I didn't mention Sundays, a day we hated as we had to dress in our "Sunday best", not daring to soil them and we weren't allowed to play. It was a relief to go to Sunday school which we enjoyed. During the summer, there was the Sunday school treat held in Platts field at Church Street when we played games and bought ice cream and sweets from the stalls. The treat really was the coach ride there and back.

The Salvation Army held magic lantern shows at the Citadel. The slides were in black and white, they didn't move and there was no talking but, no matter, they were magic.

The Saturday morning club at the Palais was the highlight of the week as we had all endured a week of suspense to see if the poor damsel in distress was to be rescued by the hero in the nick of time, all for 1d. Is it my imagination, or did the horses gallop faster and climb the high rocks with greater skill and speed than in today's westerns? What has happened to the lasso? The faster the horses galloped, the faster the music played. Occasionally a visiting artist appeared. I remember the Dagenham Girl Pipers who, after parading through the town, performed on the stage.

Mr Chinnick, the manager, was a jovial man who was often seen in the foyer distributing lollipops and, at Christmas, oranges. In 1922, when a Scouts hall was needed, he sold bricks for 6d each. £500 was needed and apparently the target was reached for the Scout hall in Acton Road is the original St Peter's Church.

There were two other cinemas, the Oxford and the Picture House.

I think of the Oxford as a long narrow building with the box office on the left-hand side near the entrance and an aisle in the centre that sloped viciously towards the screen. In 1926, Mr Roylance, a well-known musician who had a shop in Oxford Street and whose two daughters ran the Roylance school of dancing, was appointed the pianist. The rear of the cinema was in the Salts and children who decided to see the film free used to climb through the toilet window. The management became aware of this and posted an usherette outside the door. The culprit appeared and was escorted to the front entrance amid shouting and booing, not against the offender but against the usherette.

The Oxford has since been enlarged and is now a Bingo Hall.

The Picture House had a semi-circular pay office outside in the centre of the building. After you handed over 2 ½d, 5d, 8d or 1/- for a reserved seat, you received a square metal disc that made a clanging noise as it came down the chute and could be heard inside the cinema. Other distractions were the heavy curtains as they were pulled along the metal rail and the audience naturally looking to see who entered and left, the constant breaking down of the film and the applause when it resumed, and watching the cigarette smoke in the beam of light from the projector.

Mrs Payton, the manager's wife and the pianist, could be seen crossing the Rec from her home in Railway Avenue with her two Pomeranian dogs on her way to the cinema. Films were changed on Monday, Thursday and Sunday. The building is now a supermarket.

The Lawn Pavilion was another source of entertainment in a wooden hut opposite the Tankerton Hotel. The audience sat on wooden forms with their feet literally on the ground.

In 1920-21, the first council houses were built in Railway Avenue and Westmeads Road.

In 1922, there was great concern as the number of adults and schoolchildren contracting TB was on the increase.

In 1923, the Duke and Duchess of York were married. Entrance to the Palais was free that day. Normal prices were 5d, 9d, 1/3d, boxes were 2/4d , including war tax.

By 1925 the number of unemployed had decreased.

In the same year Whitstable was declared a health resort and, consequently, patients came to recuperate at holiday homes such as the Anna Wilson and St John's convalescent home. The elderly were seen in bath chairs attended by a nurse or companion. The bath chairs were wicker carriages with a large wheel at either side which was guided by the occupant with a long metal rod attached to a small front wheel. Another conveyance was the spinal carriage which looked very much like an oblong wicker basket on four wheels with the patient lying flat.

In 1926, the Whitstable and Tankerton hospital opened, a memorial to those killed in the war. It had 45 beds and cost £11,000. At that time the GPs were Witney, Etheridge, Piper, Ilderton and Barker, who was nicknamed the "salt and water doctor" because of his cure for ills such as sore throats. In the 30s, Drs Saville, Glynne, Callender, Fisher and Barker visited their patients every day as there was not a resident doctor. The visiting surgeon, Beresford Jones, was a forbidding but remarkable man. Apparently he was wounded in the foot in the war and he operated on it himself successfully without an anaesthetic although it left him with a limp.

Another hospital was the Isolation hospital. Isolation was the operative word as it was situated in a field between Whitstable and Herne Bay. It was for patients with smallpox, scarlet fever or diphtheria all of which were considered potential killers. Visitors viewed the inmates through a glass screen. In some cases, children were allowed to stay at home with the whole family in quarantine and the door of the bedroom was covered with a sheet soaked in disinfectant.

Patients suffering with TB were sent to sanitoria at Lenham, Broadstairs or Bournemouth, with the more affluent going to Switzerland, where they literally lived outside. Another condition that affected toddlers was rickets that left the child with bowed legs. Antibiotics were a thing of the future. What a boon they are. One example which happened just before the period I am talking about, in 1916, involved Mr Surman, a well-known local butcher, who collided with an employee carrying a knife which penetrated his stomach, causing peritonitis from which he subsequently died. Had he been given antibiotics he would probably have survived.

There was not a health service like today's. Doctors had private patients but for the majority, unless it was serious, it was a visit to the chemist: Iron Jelloids for anaemia, Sedlitz powders for "overheated blood", that sadistic iodine or boracic and yellow basilican ointments for cuts and grazes, Gees Linctus or Liquafruta for chesty coughs, Thermogene wadding covering back and chest like a camisole which was taken off bit by bit at the end of the winter, or brown paper soaked with vinegar placed on the forehead for headaches.

The 'flu epidemic that killed so many people.

Inoculations to my knowledge were unheard of except for vaccinations. This was compulsory unless a parent gave a valid reason to the Vaccination Officer although some dodged it. Also, before pupils were admitted to a grammar school they were forced to be vaccinated unless immunised previously and for a while wore red ribbons on their sleeves.

Insulin was discovered in 1921 and the Iron lung in 1929 - these have both saved many lives.

A large percentage of births were home births with the mother being kept in bed for two weeks. Whenever I smell Wrights Coal Tar Soap I think of newborn babies.

The school doctor visited about twice a year. There was also a nurse nicknamed Nitty Nellie who looked through the children's hair for lice and often found them.

To visit the school dentist was quite an ordeal. The charge was 1/- or 2/6d for the private dentist. False teeth were ghastly and looked like small iron railings mounted on grey vulcanite which showed when you smiled and did little to enhance your appearance. It was the same with glasses. They were not at all flattering, mostly steelrimmed. For the more fashion conscious, there were monocles for men and pince-nez for women. These were attached to a long chain worn round the neck - maybe for bad eyesight, perhaps for adornment.

There was a form of saving to ensure free hospital admittance - putting a few pence each week into a moneybox which was a replica of the local hospital.

More council houses were built in 1926 at Nos 2-24 Hamilton Road which was then an unmade road. They had the luxury of a bathroom and laid-on gas for lighting and cooking. It is interesting to note that then the Council supplied their tenants with distemper for decorating and if you took a bottle to the Council offices you were supplied with Lysol to disinfect the drains.

Private estates were built with three-bedroom houses costing £395 at a deposit of £25 with repayments of £1 a week. This seems incredible today but in the 20s it was as hard, if not harder, to find the deposit and repayments than it is today as the average wage for a manual worker was £2 10s a week or £4 for a white collar worker.

In the early 20s, we were very much under the influence of the Victorian era. I call it the dark brown era as I recall furniture, dark stained lino surrounds, brown paintwork, dark brown picture frames, rooms lit by candles or oil lamps, photographs of ancestors looking down unsmiling and resembling the wax figures at Madame Tussauds, knick-knacks on every available surface, heavy overmantle, the wood venetian blinds, the whatnot, and the aspidistra that no self-respecting family was without. I remember sitting on those sadistic horsehair chairs and couch that chaffed your legs while you went cross-eyed counting the rosebuds or something similar on the wallpaper.

Most houses consisted of a scullery, living room, parlour and three bedrooms, one of which was in the attic.

In the bedroom was a wooden or metal bed with springs, a feather mattress, sheets, blankets, pillows, bolster and bedspread, wardrobe with full-length mirror, marble-topped wash hand stand on which stood decorated china jug, washing bowl and soap dish. These were used only by visitors as the family washed at the sink in the kitchen. There was a chamber pot as the lavatory was outside. The dressing table had trinket boxes, candlesticks, hair tidy, ring holder and tray, and a tortoiseshell brush, mirror and comb.

The parlour was used only for special occasions such as weddings or, when one of the family died, the body was laid in an open coffin for friends and neighbours to pay their last respects. Until after the funeral curtains were closed along the street, the women wore black for a long time and the men had black diamonds or bands attached to the sleeves of their coats.

The living room had a large table in the centre with chairs around it with maybe a piano and treadle sewing machine, the kitchen range and a low cupboard at either side in the recess.

The scullery had a shallow sink and possibly a brick copper and shelves for heavy cast-iron saucepans, etc.

The front door led either on to the pavement or a concrete path. Great care was taken in the appearance of the house with heavy cotton lace curtains at the windows, the doorstep hearthstoned and brasses polished.

The back door led into a concrete yard. Until the late 1800s, there were wells in these yards which supplied the water and some still remain covered over. There would be a mangle, small and large zinc baths hanging on the wall and a food safe which was a wooden-framed cupboard with metal meshed sides and door. There would be an outhouse, the WC and maybe a chicken run or a rabbit hutch with any remaining space given over to flowers or vegetables. Sometimes there was a garden shed.

Surrounding the garden would be a low wooden fence and gate leading to an alley separating the houses from the next street. These were well maintained. When I see the large and small convolvulus, it reminds me of these alleys.

The tradesmen and errand boys delivering coal, groceries, etc came down these alleys. Cash was left for the rent, insurance and tallymen on the kitchen table without any fear of it being stolen.

Another memory is of Sunday mornings and the watercress and shellfish men wearing boaters and white coats and with their baskets covered by white muslin and Mr Horne the newsagent all shouting out in their peculiar lingo.

One incident I remember vividly is when I was visiting a friend and Mr Latter the tallyman was seen coming towards the houses. The word went along the alley and back doors were locked and the door remained locked or a child would call out that Mum wasn't in. On this occasion I was told to answer the door and when I told my father this I was forbidden to go to this house again. But I did!

I can recall only three men coming to the front door: the postman delivering three times a day, knocking as he left; Joe Nutten ringing a bell and delivering hot rolls at breakfast time - seven for 3d; and the milkman.

Our milkman was Mr Hudson who worked for his father-in-law, Mr Read. He delivered from an open-ended horse-drawn cart which you entered by two mobile steps. Inside there was a large metal churn from which he measured ½ or 1 pint in metal measures and poured the milk into our jugs which we covered with a round muslin cover with beads sewn around the edge or left in a metal container, not in bottles as today. He had a beautiful Old English Sheepdog (like the Dulux advert) which came with him, rain or shine. Another milkman, Mr Butcher, worked for Cottews and delivered from a hand-cart.

By the mid-twenties, the accumulator was introduced for the working of the wireless set. It was a square glass container filled with a type of acid. It was lethal and heaven help anyone who spilled it for it burned a hole in everything it touched. This was recharged once a week at a garage or wireless shop for 6d.

In 1929 the pen nib factory opened.

At the end of the 20s, we were gradually seeing changes for, although the holiday trade was booming, there was anxiety business-wise for the trades connected with the sea.

Chapter Three

THE THIRTIES

1930 to 1940 was a decade that experienced so many changes.

At the beginning Whitstable, like many other places, was not a happy town from business and employment points of view. Industries that had been the town's lifeline for years were on the decline with shipyards closing, the termination of the Winkle line for passengers, the shutdown of the furnaces of the Gas Light and Coke Company as the gas was diverted from Dover, the Palais closing in 1930 and no alternative employment. No wonder it was declared a distressed area.

The Tankerton Pavilion was opened in 1930. It had been predicted that this would bring thousands into the town and create more jobs. This turned out to be a gross exaggeration as the only section of the building used that was commercially successful was the Troc cinema. It had originally been destined to become a skating rink and stadium. It was large and spacious, seating 1000 people. Later it was divided and, after the fire, became the Embassy and closed just before the war and was taken over by the AFS as a temporary fire station.

Two chain stores opened, Boots and Woolworths, and this eased the employment situation which was appreciated by the residents but not by the small traders. Boots affected only the chemists but Woolworths, with such a variety of merchandise and with nothing costing over 6d, was another matter. They sold, among other things, hardware, cosmetics, crockery, costume jewellery (rings that turned your fingers green), eye glasses (6d each lens and 6d for the frame) and a wonderful selection of confectionery.

In 1932 the original Hamilton Mission was built by the Carnegie family with a wooden hut at the back used as a Sunday school supervised by Miss Mansell with her aunt providing tea for the pupils. The permanent building was completed in 1964.

During 1932, there was a spate of fires. First, Stanley Reeves' building yard in Warwick Road, then the Gifford family lost their home. Next Seath's timber yard in Cromwell Road, then Spenceley's draper shop in the High Street. These all happened on Wednesday nights. Anderson and Perkins shipyard and Porter's building yard in Sea Street were the next victims on Saturday nights. To my knowledge, the arsonist was not caught.

Also in 1932 the Teynham Road subway was opened by Stanley Baldwin MP. Until then, Teynham Road had been a dead end.

I believe that the Thanet Way was opened in 1934/35. It was then called the Arterial Road and bypassed Faversham through to the Thanet towns. Whether Whitstable gained by this at that time is debatable for it bypassed our town taking coaches of day trippers straight through to Thanet. It also deprived us of our lovely walks to the villages as even then it was very busy and traumatic to cross.

In 1935 the much-needed traffic lights were installed by the railway bridge. The Cycling Club was formed by Squib Whorlow and meetings were held in the hall at the back of Webb's newspaper shop in the High Street. The Club was disbanded in 1940 as members were called up.

In 1934, the giraffe-necked women from Penang Thailand visited. They were appearing in a circus in Canterbury and crowds gathered as they left the Bear and Key Hotel.

We were becoming aware of the aeroplane, probably because of the achievements of Lindbergh, Erhardt and Amy Johnson. Folk were so thrilled that a song was written about Amy.

Alan Cobham gave flying displays at Pouts field at Chestfield and also took passengers up. The machines were crude in comparison with today's planes, twin winged with a propeller. The passenger and pilot were unprotected from the elements - to many people this was wonderful but frightening.

In 1935, the old Oxford cinema, affectionately known as The Flea Pit, was demolished and the new building which seated over 800 was built. The Picture House closed and was renamed the Argosy.

We celebrated King George's Silver Jubilee with a holiday. A number of festivities were held were held in the main venue, the Rec. Children were presented with mugs and medals and there was "a bag tea for the children and a dug out tea for the unemployed". I have yet to find out what a dug out tea means. There was also a procession and a firework display.

Owing to the abdication of Edward VIII 326 days after his succession, we celebrated the coronation of King George and Queen Elizabeth with the same festivities but with a very important addition - it was shown on television in black and white. Mr Gaywood, the wireless and television retailer, opened his Tankerton shop and gave the first public showing.

The Castle grounds were opened to the public. They boasted a fine bowling green, open-air dances were held in the rose garden and the castle became the home of the Urban District Council.

The wireless was becoming a must in the home. It was operated by an accumulator or, for those fortunate enough to have electricity, by the mains for the 2 or 3 valve sets. Mr Gaywood collected and returned the accumulators to outlying districts until the war for 6d.

Programmes from the Continent were received from stations such as Luxembourg, Paris, Hilversum, Brussels etc. Donald Piers, broadcasting from Luxembourg in his Sunday morning show, was singing his current hit "By a babbling brook". When my father heard this he told me to "turn that row off". I wonder what he would have said about today's hit tunes?

Thanks to the cinema and wireless, the outlook on life had broadened. Also, labour-saving devices were becoming more accessible, such as fires, iron, cookers and coppers, gas and electric. The New World gas cooker, fitted with the Regulo thermostat, became so popular that cookery demonstrations were held at the Masonic Hall.

Gas lighting had its ups and downs. Air in the pipes caused the light to fade and flicker, making a plop plop sound that meant the pipes needed to be "blown out". Do you remember placing the fragile Sugg or Veritas mantle into the three grooves on the holder, replacing the globe carefully and trying hard not to break the mantle and then screwing it onto the fitting? What an ordeal. And those awful geysers and the verdigris deposits.

Many homes and newly-built houses had electricity installed, enabling vacuum cleaners as well as other labour-saving devices to be purchased. It was a luxury to have a radiogram.

New houses were built and newlyweds in particular took advantage of these.

Light wood furniture replaced the heavy dark oak of the 20s. There were fewer knick knacks, there was chromium plate on furniture, frameless mirrors and picture frames, enamel kitchenware - a popular make, Judge, was obtainable in blue, red, green and cream and was such a contrast to the cast iron pans used on the kitchener. The kitchener was not installed in the new houses. In its place was a gas or electric stove in the kitchen and an open fire, with tile surround, in the living and sitting rooms. The wash hand stand was no longer included in the bedroom suites, carpets replaced lino squares and lino on the stairs and we had the Ewbank carpet sweeper.

Such things as the kitchener, venetian blinds and the aspidistra were things of the past with freezers, fridges, food mixers and microwaves things of the future.

As I have said, the holiday trade was booming with visitors and commercial travellers using the hotels and furnished flats and houses were let for the summer season. There were more privately owned cars on the roads, telephones were installed for both business and residential use, and the wireless programmes were becoming more varied as they transmitted from Daventry and London and from venues other than the studio.

George Fitt had a secondhand car pound opposite his garage at Tankerton Circus. For a mere £2.10s you could become the proud owner of an aptly named bone shaker. Men tried to mechanise their cycles by fixing a motor on the carrier above the back wheel - the craze didn't last.

The East Kent Road Car Company had the monopoly of passenger road services. I'm aware of two companies who tried to provide a service but failed - they were Fred Fitt and the Grampian Car Company.

The Southern Railway provided an excellent services. Typical fares were as follows. If you fancied a day's trip to London, providing you were at the station by 5.30am to travel on the milk (or was it the paper) train, you would pay 1/2d return to Chatham and then dash across to the booking office to pay another 1/2d to London, a total of 2/4d.

I felt that around 1937 life in general was improving (unemployment figures were down, the building trade was on the up, life for the housewife was less arduous) but it was politically unsettling with so much conflict, the Spanish Civil War, the Invasion of Abyssinia by Italy, Heads of State and royalty being dethroned or murdered in Europe, Fascist Moseley and his disciples (who were called the Black

Shirts although the local uniform was brown) parading around. Here we did not experience the terrorism that was found in the East End of London. Even with Hitler becoming more powerful, we still rejected the idea that we would be drawn into another war. This belief was cemented when in 1938 Chamberlain came back from Munich waving that famous piece of paper and assuring us all was well. How naive and trusting we were. Later on, with the distribution of identity cards and gas masks, we then felt very ill at ease. Then came the mobilisation of the Navy and on 3 June 1939 the first registration of men aged 20-21 and in July those aged 19 were conscripted.

On the night of 2 September, we experienced our first blackout and the testing of the siren at midday.

On 2 September, I was a bridesmaid at All Saints Church. My father came to see the wedding and was hijacked into taking some evacuees from Chatham, seven in all. He hadn't registered to do so but apparently some who had did not turn up. When I arrived home, having walked along Stream Walk to Church Road alone in the pitch black in the early hours of the morning, I was quite unaware of the visitors and, not daring to put on the light, I fell over bodies in every room. The only vacant space was the kitchen table which was not the comfiest of beds but, having celebrated well, it didn't worry me! In the morning, between putting up heavy curtains, etc, we listened to every news bulletin still hoping, right up to the deadline of 11 o'clock when what we all feared was confirmed, ironically just after the siren sounded. ARP wardens rushed around ushering everyone into the nearest house, not knowing what to expect and remembering the awful bombing before the occupation of the European countries. Luckily it was a false alarm - one of ours.

This is where my story ends as I took the 2.30 train to live and work in Highbury, North London, for better or worse, I knew not.

Never again would life be the same. The six families owning a TV set would have to put it in store for the duration. For others, those on the home front would experience a different way of life, women on war work became independent, others joined the forces or were sent to other parts of England and married there, whilst those at home married lads billeted in the town. Thank goodness we did not know what was in store for us. Even civilians were not exempt from the killings and maiming.

Here's hoping that in future we will see the warning signs and endeavour to avoid another such catastrophe.

Chapter Four

THE SEASONS

Whitstable, like most seaside towns, came alive around Easter, hopeful of a good season ahead.

Restaurants and hotels took on temporary staff, pleasure and fishing boats were overhauled and painted, huts were refurbished, bazaars re-stocked and one must not forget the holiday landlady who welcomed holidaymakers. Often the same families came year after year and her house would have been spring-cleaned and the appropriate cards such as 'Bed and Breakfast' and 'Board Residence' placed in the front window. Everything was ready, turning the home into a mini-boarding house with visitors taking the best rooms and the family banished to the back rooms and attics. All that was needed was a hot dry summer for there were few activities should it be cold and wet.

On Palm Sunday, children were given crosses made from palm leaves and on Maundy Thursday they walked crocodile fashion from school to church. After the service, they were dismissed to start a ten-day holiday. Good Friday was a solemn day. The shops and cinemas were closed and the children were not allowed out to play.

On Easter Sunday morning we were awakened by the Salvation Army playing 'Christ the Lord has risen today'. Sadly this is no longer heard. Children attended Sunday School and Church, for teenagers a different venue. It was virtually an Easter Parade, more so in the Thirties, from the High Street to Tankerton Beach. It was the day new outfits were worn regardless of the weather. How we girls suffered having discarded warm clothing. There is a saying that pride feels no pain. Untrue! And so speaks one from hard experience.

On Easter Monday, families walked or cycled to the woods, maybe Clover Rise or Radfall or until 1930 to South Street or Tyler Hill on the railway for a few pence. Weather permitting, they gathered primroses, violets, pussy willow and possibly bluebells. Children gathered wild flowers on the railway banks - this is not possible today, not only because of the danger factor but also because it is illegal, I believe.

In the thirties, the car became more accessible, enabling folk to travel further afield. Also there were organised events.

Gypsies called at houses and stood in the main streets with babies lashed to their bodies by strips of material or scarves. They sold homemade pegs, bunches of violets and primroses and baskets made from thick twigs and filled with primrose roots. Again, this is now illegal.

Mothering Sunday was not observed as it is today although the Salvation Army gave the children one flower to take home - a lovely gesture.

Boat Race Saturday was always great fun. Emblems in various shapes were bought for ½d and had ribbons denoting the crew you supported. There was great rivalry and the results appeared in the evening papers and were announced on the wireless. In the thirties, you heard it on the Pathe news.

Restaurants, amusements and pleasure boats opened or operated at weekends until Whitsun.

Children went back to school until Whitsun and St George's Day, 23 April, was celebrated by a pageant depicting the slaying of the dragon by St George.

On May Day, girls wearing garlands in their hair danced round the Maypole. On Empire Day, 24 May, a senior pupil appeared as Britannia in all her glory. (As Commonwealth Day this was recognised on the Queen's official birthday, 12 June). These were not holidays and to my knowledge the only one upheld today is the dancing round the maypole. One year I remember that for an Empire Day 'do' a Madame Burgess (Mrs Jupp) had the unenviable task of forming a choir to sing 'Land of Hope and Glory'. I cannot remember if she was successful or not but every time I hear that song I think of her doing her best with such a crowd of unlikely choristers.

From Whitsun onwards, the town and seafront were getting busier by the week and by the end of July the season was in full swing until 1930 while the Winkle Line was operating and bringing visitors from Canterbury and elsewhere. If they weren't staying, they came as day trippers as the Southern Railway service was frequent and reasonably priced.

Whitstable was very popular as it was advertised as a health resort, the nearest town from London and the Medway towns with safe bathing, unspoiled seafront and lovely countryside.

Until 1960 both booking offices were functioning with trains from London arriving and passengers passing through the barrier. At the one which is now closed, visitors were met by an army of young lads with home-made carts to take luggage and owners to their holiday abode for the cost of a few coppers. Foremans and Dunks' Taxis waited outside with a ride to anywhere in the town costing one shilling.

Families came year after year, often to the same landlady and, having settled in, they naturally made their way to the beaches.

Tankerton Beach, having more amusements than the others, was the most popular, especially for children and teenagers. Walking to the harbour which would be full of barges, ships and yachts, you could see boys diving into the harbour and railways trucks being pulled along to the turntables by horses. Pedestrians and traffic halted at the level crossing from the station to the harbour and you crossed over to Tower Parade as the path ended at the harbour gates. So on to the beach, stopping at Jacques to try your luck on the machines and look at the 'naughty postcards' which caused so much laughter.

On to Mrs Holmes for an ice cream or to one of the tea houses for a cuppa and then collecting buckets, spades, waterwings and those ghastly multi-coloured sun hats with fringed brims from Dadds or Malnicks. Then, past Ted Humphries' swing boats and collecting a deck chair to watch the activities out at sea - vessels in and out of the harbour or speedboats skimming the water at a terrific speed. Mr and Mrs Court and Walters stood on the boat pier enticing folk to take a trip around the oyster beds for 2/- on the dressed overall Moss Rose or the Rose Marie (she helped at Dunkirk and is now in Malta).

You might also see Lappy Horn with his Hokey Pokey barrow. At one time Lappy had been the Town Crier which is remarkable as he could neither read nor write but he had a good memory.

In the Thirties, Mr Offredi turned the house next door to his restaurant into the Hotel Continental where tea dances were held on the ground floor until the outbreak of war. These have not been resumed.

Apparently in the Twenties goat shades stood along the sea front giving rides for 1d but I don't remember this.

Opposite, a large frame displayed photographs taken the previous day by photographers mingling with the crowds.

A favourite amusement was Mr Griggs' bubbles. This was a rectangular stall and for 1d you received a long rod attached to a metal net placed against a funnel in the centre. A foot-operated bellow sent the table tennis balls to the top and the first person to catch three received a box of Sharps Toffees or a bar of chocolate. After a while you became wise and stood where the breeze caught the balls!

Going farther along you passed the huts, all named and occupied with portable gramophones playing the latest tunes and women wearing gaily coloured beach pyjamas. Dawes cafe on the Slopes was always busy and on Sundays brass bands, such as the Black

Dyke colliery and St Hilda's played in the bandstand. The Lawn Pavilion provided shows in the afternoon and evening. Hotels such as the Marine Cafe Royal and Tankerton were popular with the equivalent of today's Hooray Henries.

Visitor to Tankerton could show a copy of the News Chronicle to Lobby Ludd and say "You are Lobby Ludd and I claim the News Chronicle's prize (10/-)". This was profitable for the newsagents and not so good for the lookalikes.

The Troc opened in 1930. The Castle grounds with its bowling green were also opened to the public and dances were held in the rose garden in 1935.

Although Tankerton beaches drew the crowds and locals enjoyed walking along what I call the Bottom Prom, it was beaches such as Reeves and the West beaches that were most frequented, particularly by those with young children. At Reeves Beach, before the sea wall was built, there was a sparsely grassed slope which was great fun for running down to the beach and passing mothers who were keeping an eagle eye on the children, people talking to friends and perhaps enjoying a picnic. You used to cringe as the pebbles hurt your feet as few people possessed paddling shoes. The girls tucked their dresses into their knickers and the boys rolled up their trouser legs as they floated toy boats, skimmed the water at full tide with flat shells, collected cockles and winkles to take home to cook, played games when the tide went out. I noticed large holes which had been dug for bait close to the beach. This is very dangerous for children as they are not visible when the tide is in. They used to be dug farther out and I wonder if you still need a licence to dig?

Older folk sat on the seats watching the sea traffic coming round the Ness and heading for the harbour, the fishing and oyster fleet and the paddle steamer from Southend to Herne Bay. Apparently in the early Twenties there was a skating rink with a cafe above. During the summer holidays, Sunshine Corner was great fun for the young with games, competitions and a singsong on the beach if it was fine or in the Methodist Church in Albert Street if it was wet. Of an evening, artists could be seen following in the footsteps of Turner and Sherrin as they tried to capture the magnificent spectacle of the sunset that Whitstable is famous for - along with the oysters.

West Beach was always crowded as the houses around accommodated visitors, the huts were let and the boating lake, tennis courts and the Red Spider cafe were popular venues for teenagers.

The carnivals of 1921, 22 and 23 were disappointing as they were held on a Monday. Also in 1924, 25 and 26 they were held on the Monday evening of the day of the regatta followed by a firework display. From 1927-39, they were held on a Wednesday, separated by a week from the regatta. By the late Twenties, the carnival was well supported and considered the best along our coast with an average of 150 entries. The subject and design of the entries, particularly the solo ones, was jealously guarded with people spending weeks on their creations. For those needing vans or lorries, the timing was difficult as the vehicles were used until midday but then it was all hands on the job with everyone praying that it would not rain as the majority of the decorations were of crepe paper.

In 1932 we had our first Carnival Queen who was chosen at a dance organised by the IMPS at the Parish Hall. In following years she was chosen on August Bank holiday on the Slopes followed by community singing led by Alan Ratcliffe - The Man in White of the News Chronicle - which he finished with 'Abide With Me' saying it was Queen Mary's favourite hymn.

Many of the floats were humorous with everyone joining in the fun. The procession started from Cromwell Road and on to the Tollgate turning and finishing at Priest and Sow. Then there was dancing on the Green (in 1935 this was in the Castle grounds - on concrete). Afterwards we walked home, a traumatic business as youths laden with bags of confetti attacked the girls by emptying them down the fronts of their dresses and bumping them up and down. Arriving home we had to undress in the yard and remnants of this remained on our underclothes and skin for some time as the colour of the confetti stained. This doesn't happen anymore as the fights were banned when they got out of hand.

CARNIVAL QUEENS AND ATTENDANTS

	Queens	Attendants
1932	Kelly Day	Lillian Barham Dorothy Spence
1933	Dorothy Spence	Kelly Day
1934	Kelly Day	Dorothy Spence Gwenda King
1935	Edith Bean	Joan Hinton Innes Phyllis Harnett Ida Rawlins
1936	Ivy Revell	V Entwistle Doris Ashby Joan Wellard
1937	Queenie Revell	E Faulkner W Hadler F Waters S Allen
1938	Mary Fell	Pauline Mitchell Winifred Hadler Queenie Revell
1939	Patricia Bean	Joan Cooley Ivy Revell Bunty Young

The Queen's float created by Harold Wilson was superb. He did this for years and his son followed on, keeping up the tradition.

There was another carnival - called Dan Sherrin's Seasalter Carnival - held just once in the Twenties consisting of one float by the Seasalter Slow Stew Company Ltd who distributed leaflets with recipes for Seasalter sparrow pie soup and fillets of fish pie. This was Dan Sherrin up to his usual unpredictable actions.

Next came the regatta with competitions such as swimming, yacht racing, the greasy pole and so on. The highlight was the bombardment of the judges' barge with soot and flour by Alan Cobham's flying circus with his team standing on the wings of the plane flying very low over the beaches and town. In 1935 the Graf Zeppelin flew over while the regatta was in progress. There was also another regatta held at West Beach, organised by the Sea Scouts, with events such a lemon cutting, treacle roll and duck hunt contests. Sadly, I can't find any information on these.

A number of shows took place - sports days, gymkhanas and the Fur and Feather Show - at first in the Rec and later in the Belmont Ground.

Also there were fairs and circuses held in Warwick Road until the houses were built there and then on the Salts. The fairs consisted of a number of amusements - chairoplanes, the Hall of Mirrors, the caterpillar, to mention just a few and many sideshows with numerous prizes. An example was a display board with names of towns on it in the middle of the stall with a light at the back which moved up and down and then stopped. The person with the winning ticket - costing 3d - then chose a prize. Our household was kept supplied with tea services from this source.

Well-known circuses came - Sangers, Bertram Mills, Barnetts and the Wild West Show were wonderful and spectacular. So many artistes, clowns, acrobats, stilt men, tightrope walkers, horses, elephants, camels and Shetland ponies. This was two hours of fun and excitement though some acts were frightening, for example, the tightrope walkers pretending to fall and trapeze artistes missing their partners who fell into the safety net. They were _real_ circuses. After the Big Top was erected, the artistes and animals paraded through the town stopping at the Horsebridge to paddle.

A story is told about one circus. Apparently it was the custom for one elephant to call at Mr Sawyer's bakehouse in Bexley Street on its way to Warwick Road for a bun or two. On this occasion, Mr Sawyer was not there and the scared assistant hit him. On the next visit this elephant, on seeing the assistant, put his trunk around him and bashed him against the wall. They say an elephant never forgets but whether this story is true or not, I don't know - it was told to me by a sailor!

The Boating Lake opening in the mid-Thirties by Mr Scammel. It was popular with visitors and residents alike and golf contests were held in the adjoining field. Closing it deprived us of another facility.

There were clubs and societies, the Homing, Operatic, Waifs and Strays, football, golf, tennis and cricket.

Dances were held regularly at the Drill, Masonic, Foresters and Parish Halls and in the main hotels. They lasted longer than today's dances, often from 7.30pm until 2.00am. We danced to Norman Perkins, George Dunn, the Royal Native Jazz and the Municipal Jazz bands, dances such as streamer, flannel and masked which are not heard of today.

During the summer there were a number of fires on the railway banks which had been ignited by sparks from the trains, haystacks in the fields from combustion. The maroon sounded and Tom Rigden who was in charge and later W Fisher, and Mr Poole the watchmaker, Lawson the cabinet maker, Wyver from the waterworks, Moyse the postman, Blythe, Savage and Camburn all rushed to the fire station on their bikes in record time. These were dedicated men, all volunteers who followed their occupations during the day. For us children it was great fun following the engine on our bikes - it would be impossible to do this today. The roads were gritted and tarred, levelled off by an enormous steam roller, and were not appreciated by the cyclists as the grit punctured the tyres.

Street vendors, the knife grinders complete with sharpening stone on his barrow, the barrel organ which was a favourite of mine, with or without a monkey, the rag and bone man who actually paid you for rags, newspapers and unwanted household goods, the Walls' ice-cream man on a tricycle with a square blue box between two large wheels with the logo 'Stop me and buy one'. Do you remember the triangular-shaped sno-fruit that cost 1d?

There were street singers, and one I particularly remember came regularly year after year, tall, thin, wearing a raincoat, bowler hat and boots that looked too big and heavy for him. He walked in the middle of the road, always singing 'Abide With Me' - the rendering grim. He came from Faversham and it is said that he died leaving property and thousands of pounds.

The end of the season is now here. Tearooms and restaurants are closed, the boats are brought to the top of the beach and covered with tarpaulin, huts vacated, visitors gone. Thankfully we have said goodbye to the Fresh Air Kids who for some years until 1939 arrived from the East End of London each summer. Local residents dreaded them coming. To us country yokels they were worldly, cocky and streetwise. Some were well behaved but many were wild and unruly. Some had head lice and weren't toilet trained. Hosts were paid 11/- a week and there were three batches of two weeks each. Some said that they should have been paid danger money. Having had them for one year, many refused to have them again as they vandalised property, raided gardens and fought with the local children. My father, the lamplighter, had to constantly replace glass and mantles in the lamps.

One year in the North of England a doctor murdered his wife and children's nanny. The Fresh Air Kids sang a song to the tune of 'Red Sails in the Sunset':
> "Red stains on the carpet
> Red stains on your knife
> Oh, Dr Buck Ruxton, you murdered your wife,
> Your maid, Mary, saw you,
> You thought she would tell,
> So Dr Buck Ruxton you killed her as well".

In comparison, the boys at the Shaftesbury Home at Seasalter were well behaved and disciplined.

By now the children had gone back to school except those who went hop-picking with their families. Hopping was a working holiday and means of making cash to help finances during the coming winter so they went every year for about three weeks to fields at Dargate, Boughton and Herne Hill.

Horses and carts and vans arrived to take the families and the essentials for the stay in the allotted hut which was sparse but adequate with no bed, only straw to sleep on, and a communal hut for cooking and washing. They worked long hours for the more bins that were filled the greater the wage packet.

Their produce came from the farmer but I suspect that many a rabbit or chicken met their doom from the young lads.

The get-together of an evening was fun, meeting up with old friends and mixing with the Londoners, picking the hops and, over the goodbyes, promising to meet again next year, God willing.

Back at home, the children were in school and the households returned to normality. Harvest Festival was the next celebration when we attended church with offerings of garden produce. Apart from walking in the woods and gathering chestnuts, conkers and hazel nuts, very little happened.

On the first Monday in October, Trades Day, shops closed and traders and assistants enjoyed the organised trips to Cadbury at Bourneville or to Huntley and Palmers at Reading. The Aldershot Tattoo was another event. None of these takes place now.
The build-up to Christmas was exciting. Shops did not display or dress the windows until the end of November and each had its own identity - Daly's the grocers had one window filled with a fantastic show of crackers and tins of biscuits and the other with wooden boxes of uncut candied peel, glace fruit and pudding fruits. Daniels and Collars and Miss Kemps were stacked with toys. Gambrills, the

little shop in Harbour Street, sold a large selection of edible tree decorations. One I remember was a bird in a cage - by the time the sugar was detached from the net cage, there was little to eat. Also the pink and white mice and pigs and many more.

We took the Christmas cake to Smiths the baker to be cooked for 2/6d (I am told he would also cook the Sunday joint). Late in December the poultry was hanging in the butcher's window and a large showing of fruit in Knowles.

Prize-giving, the rehearsal of the Sunday and day school plays, plus the school party all added to the excitement as the time had now come to break up for the holiday, collect holly and make paper chains.

On Christmas morning the Salvation Army paraded the streets playing 'Christians awake, salute this happy morn' - sadly this doesn't happen any more. For the poor children in the town the Carnegie family provided a meal named the robin's breakfast at the Assembly Hall.

After Christmas came the round of parties and, for the adults, the firm's dinner and dance. There were also dances from New Year's Eve until Twelfth Night.

The children went back to school.

Winters were severe. It was not uncommon to skate on the dyke running through the golf links or to toboggan on Duncan Down. For the unfortunate folks living in the lower part of the town, there was always the fear of flooding. To these, the sea wall has been a blessing although it has spoiled the appearance of the seafront. There is one thing we can be sure of on our coast and that is the N-NE bitterly cold winds.

So, roll on Easter.

Chapter Five

THINGS I REMEMBER

1. At the top of the list must be the Salvation Army band playing at the top of Albert Street on Saturday evening, marching from the Cross to the Citadel on Sunday evening, playing carols at Christmas and hymns at Easter.

2. Walking along Reeves Beach, eating and enjoying my 1d of chips.

3. Going into Miss Griffiths' shop for ½d prize bag by making a cone of newspaper which she filled with a variety of sweets.

4. Sherbet dabs, lemonade powder, Barratto juice and locust beans.

5. Walking along Tankerton Front after dark alone or with a friend without fear.

6. Of an evening, walking along the High Street, boys wolf-whistling and hoping for a pick up, passing Spenceleys that has showcases unseen from the pavement, boys taking their current girlfriend for a 'spoon' between the showcases.

7. The bottles of different flavoured minerals that could only be opened by releasing a marble in the neck of the bottle by a dome-shaped opener with a prong in the centre.

8. Old Mother Riley (a man from Ramsgate) coming year after year to the carnival collecting for local charities.

9. Miss Court as Britannia every year.

10   Leaving the house unlocked and unattended with monies left for the tradesmen to collect.

11   Purchasing an item in a drapery shop and if a ¼d change was required being given a strip of pins instead of the cash.

12   Intrigued by the method of paying for goods at the Co-op or Daveys. The assistant placed the cash and invoice into a small container attached to a contraption overhead, pulled a lever and it whizzed along wires to the cash desk and returned by the same method with change and receipt. For years I have wondered what this gadget was called and thanks to Les Rogers I now know it was a Lamson's Rapid Cash Carrier.

13   The small shops lit with candles.

14   The ½d clay pipe from Ewings to blow bubbles.

15   The smell of the grocer's shop, bladders of lard and sides of bacon hanging, large blocks of butter, lard and cheese, watching the assistant using butter pats.

16   Those awful sticky flycatchers.

17   The Darren Bread delivery van shaped as a brown loaf.

18   Having condensed milk, not fresh, in the tea.

19   Miss Ethel dressed in white with a yellow beret advertising Ethel petrol.

20   Cutting paper into small squares and stringing them together to use as toilet paper.

21   My grandmother cooking buns on Sunday morning and my cousins and I waiting to sample them.

22   The fascination of watching the trucks on the harbour taken to the turntables by the horses.

23   Carts drawn by dray horses which on special occasions displayed highly polished brasses.

24   To be chosen as ink monitor at school, pens with nibs were used, not ballpoints like today. Such a privilege!

25   Watching my father filling the bicycle lamp with a mixture of water and carbide - a foul smelling substance that produced a gas ignited by a match.

26   When Ex-Lax came on to the market, samples were put through letter boxes. As people did not read the instructions before eating it, you can imagine the consequences!

27   Having slices of bread and dripping for Sunday tea - spreading the beef jelly from the Sunday joint on to the bread. Delicious.

28   The ceasing of the organ at the Congregational Church as the lad operating the bellows had fallen asleep. Hymns were sung to the accompaniment of moans and groans from the organ.

29   The Troc held a contest to choose a Shirley Temple lookalike. Obviously these poor eight year-olds had to sleep in curlers the night before as straight hair was miraculously turned into ringlets.

30   Felix the cat that kept on walking. The annuals and flicker books which, if flicked quickly, demonstrated how fast he walked.

31   The atmosphere from the Winkle line station along to Tankerton Beach on a hot summer day.

32   Clip-on metal false handles for cups.

33   Pot menders similar to large washers.

34   The smell of mothballs in the wardrobe impregnating everything hanging inside.

35   Shoes that had been patched.

36   Bookies' runners discreetly taking bets in the pubs or on the street. This was illegal and if they were caught the result was a heavy fine.

37   Women running along the back alleys with a jug for the pint of stout from the bottle and jug bar at their local.

OLDEST RAILWAY BRIDGE IN THE WORLD, TANKERTON

Chapter Six

SNIPPETS FROM 'THE WHITSTABLE TIMES'

1920 Divorcée no longer bound to cohabit with husband.
War memorial unveiled by Lord Harris.
350 tons of Dutch cheese arrived at the harbour.
Jam jars wanted - ½d for 1lb and 2lb, 1d for 3lb. Each child bringing a jar will be given a toy.
House waste bones wanted - 9d per lb.
No street lamps to be lit in June.
Advertisement for carpet beating factory.
Production up as smoking was allowed.
Rode cycle from Dover to France - amazing!

1922 Extension of Tankerton sea wall undertaken as relief work for the unemployed. Pay 9d per hour - they struck for more.

1923 Post Office stated that wireless sets should not be taken house from house.
Man sentenced for being drunk - a dealer of the lower class.
Mr Chinnick refused the lease of bandstand.
Lighting up for cyclists and others.

1924 Site purchased for lavatories and other purposes.
Man fined for speeding at 25 miles an hour.

1926 Man fell down and expired.
Music lessons by Madam Royland, who described herself as "a pupil of William Shakespeare".
Child lassooed from train.
500 Everdry chairs bought by the council.
Man charged for stealing a box of Oxos (6d).

1927　Bus conductor killed by hitting his head on lamp-post when looking out from the platform.
First photograph of a wedding in The Times.
New ambulance dedicated by Rev. Long.
Opening of the Shaftesbury Home.
Baby dies through overlaying.

1928　First account of divorce.
Series of fund-raising events and an appeal for outstanding debt of £39.9.5d for People's Free Mission.
Guest at wedding gave lino and razor (presumably to cut the lino).
Scarcity of milk means price rise to 7d per quart.
Man to pay 2/6d per week towards maintenance of mental home.
Man confirmed dead as life was extinct.

1930　Whitstable Boys' Naval Brigade renamed Sea Cadets.
Man divested himself of coat and shoes.

1932　Three men murdered at Swalecliff.

1933　34 cars in treasure hunt.

1935　Swalecliff zoo proprietor - suicide by shooting.

1938　Artificial teeth wanted - 2s-10s a tooth.

SECTION TWO

Whitstable

Chapter Seven

WARTIME

A PLACE FOR THEM

We'll keep a place for them

In our memory.

This town was home for them

And will always be.

In our minds, young are they,

Unflawed by cruel time.

Yours and mine are they,

Of Whitstable's line.

John Daniels
9 October 1993

WAR CASUALTIES 1914-1918

Adams W
Allen F W
Allen G E
Allen A J
Ames E
Andrews A J
Andrews J R
Appleton A E
Appleton A S
Appleton C H
Appleton F
Baker J
Barham T F
Barton J A
Barton S
Bashford W H
Beard C
Beckhuson D J
Bentley C C
Bentley C T
Bisson A T
Blaxland E M
Botting D
Brehart J J
Brett W R
Browning F A
Burton C H
Bull W
Bunce J F
Callup F H E
Camburn F C
Candy W H
Capon O
Carden E G
Carpenter C
Carruthers D P
Castle H J
Charrington D
Church F M P

Clark C
Clark W G
Clark W J
Clarringbold E A
Clothier F C
Clothier W
Clothier W H
Cole C
Cole J
Coleman R
Collar A V
Collar P H
Coombs W
Cornhill A R
Cosling A W
Curling C N
Deverson B C
Down F W
Duncan F
Dunkley E
Dyson ?
Elkin W J
Evans E R
Fisher A J
Foad A
Foad S J
Foad W B
Foreman W H
Foreman T
Forster W E B
Fox E A
Gambrell A S
Graves A H
Greenwell A W
Griffey E
Hadlow J F
Haggett H E
Halliday W
Hampshire E

Harlow T H
Harman R
Harris A E R
Harris W
Harrison E G
Harvey E W
Hawkins A
Hemsley M S
Herbert L E
Hill A E
Horne H
Hudson A
Hudson J S
Hulkes E
Hurlock A
Hunt J A
Janes L F
Johns F
Jones C
Johnstone R J
Jordan C W
Keam B
Keam C J
Knight R E
Lawson A
Longhurst C
Lott F C
MacKenzie C A
Madams J
Mantle R C
Marsh F J
Matthews H
Maxted A
May H R P F
Mitchell D
Morgan P
Mummery A
Nazer F J
Norman W C

Norris A E
Nye C W
Olive R
Orpin H
Packman T
Parnham J R
Paul D
Payne A
Payne H
Pellett H B
Pepper J W T
Phillips H
Philpott R S
Picott R
Picott R
Prescott J
Price A W
Richards H
Richards FW
Rickwood C A

Rigden C C
Rigden H
Rigden H A
Rigden H C
Rowden S C
Sandy W E
Saunders F
Saunders W C
Sharp F T O
Silk C W
Smith C G
Smithson P W
Souter F C
Speed F J
Steer H J
Stroud R E
Stroud W
Stroud W
Strand A
Stupple C

Tappenden T W
Taylor F
Thompsett F
Thompson R E J
Tinley J
Tranter E S
Tresize O
Uden H
Uden W M S
Vaughan W M J
Warwick C G
Webb H
Widdett J
Whitmore E
Whorlow C J M
Wood A G
Wootton J F
Wyles W
Wyver G

WAR CASUALTIES 1939 - 1945 (Service Personnel)

Ball G
Bashford F
Beeching L
Beck A
Bisson A
Blackbourne B
Bradley E
Burns G
Blyth G T
Borrough J H
Camburn E
Chesman W
Copping W E
Couchman W
Cowie V
Croft RP
Currey R
Davey T

De Boughn J
Dowman P
Fairbrass A E
Field P R
Finch G
Finch J
Fisher J
Fogg L
Fogg W
Foreman F
Flynn W
Gambrill A
Garrod J R
Garston P
Gaylard G
Gaylard P C
Gillam F C
Gummett P J

Gummett P
Harrison Stupple J
Holmes E H H
Holmes N T
Hook E
James F
Jarratt E
Jones A
Joiner F
Keam H
Keam S
Keast F J
Keele K
Kenningham D
King D
Laker N
Laraman W
Lefevre P

Lowdnes F
Maflin L
Marler E
Merritt V
Meteyard S
Midas V A
Miles F C
Milham V J
Mitchell D
Morgan B
Moss G L
Mount C
Mummery S A
Munnock A R
Nathan EW
Newman A W
Olive R E
Packman L
Palmer L
Pitt V

Pizzey L
Powell H
Prett S
Quinn P
Reed N
Rowden H
Rowden J H
Rowden V
Sampson W E
Saunders L
Seath P
Snelling S
Spratt G
Steele J
Stephens M
Stephenson G
Stott A
Stroud F
Stroud R R
Sugden A

Surtees A
Swire W
Sykes D C
Tilley S
Tritton A L
Tutt C J
Wallis Stolze R
Waitt E C
Walsh B J
Waters C B
Whorlow F W
Wilks C A
Wilkie E C
Williams A A F
Williams E
Williams E
Williams J
Witney P
Wood G
Woodward W
Wraight A

CIVILIANS

Barton S (ARP)
Barton A M
Collingham J W
Daniels W
Day D V

Frend D E
Frend D M
Frend J
Garrod J (HG)
Paget S (HG)

Palmer L A (HG)
Rigden S
Spellen J N (HG)
Tilley E M
Williams M I (ARP)

Names were supplied to The Whitstable Improvement Trust in 1996 to complete their list for the 1939 -1945 memorial.

Chapter Eight

WHITSTABLE PEOPLE

CELEBRITIES

Charlie Chester - entertainer - (1914 - 1997)

Charlie was born in Eastbourne in 1914 and has lived in Chestfield for a number of years. In 1989, he celebrated his Golden Wedding with his wife, Dorita, who he met when they were both appearing in the show 'Silly Isn't It?' at Bromley. They had one son.

A very well-known artiste, his many long-running radio shows included 'Keep Smiling', 'Come to Charlie' and 'A Proper Charlie' as well as his current show, 'Sunday Soapbox' which has run for the last 21 years.

His TV appearances included 'Pot Luck' (the first TV giveaway show), 'Charlie Chester Music Hall', 'I Object' and 'Those Were The Days'. He also wrote and starred 'A Sparrow in Fleet Street'.

He had done virtually everything in showbiz - films, farce, Shakespeare, pantomime and Royal Command performances.

A songwriter of hit tunes, he concentrated on military band music and songs for choirs and he wrote fiction and non-fiction books, including poetry and crime novels. He was in demand as an after-dinner speaker.

Charlie was a past King Rat, the youngest since Dan Leno, and he held the office of Poet Laureate to the Grand Order.

He was awarded the MBE and the Order of St John for his work for charity which included a one-man art exhibition which raised a considerable sum of money.

After Dorita died, Charlie married a family friend, Joan.
Charlie died in 1997 at Brinscombe House, the Actors nursing home, aged 83.

A memorial service with full honours was held at St Martins in the Fields.

Peter Cushing - actor - (1913-1994)

If I were to write a complete history of this gentleman - gentleman being the operative word - I would need pages and pages plus many hours to do him justice, so let me try to give a brief account of his life.

He was born in Kenley, Surrey, later moving to Dulwich village. At the kindergarten there he made an appearance as a pixie. It is amazing to associate this small boy - whose mother wanted a daughter and therefore clothed him in dresses and tied pink ribbons in his hair - with the man who in later life played such gruesome characters as Dracula and Frankenstein.

He entered Shoreham Grammar School for one term and then went to Purley County School - an unwilling student, good at sport and acting in school plays. On leaving school, he worked as a surveyor's assistant but, frustrated with that, he applied to entry to the Guildhall School of Music and Drama where the interviewer said, "Take that boy away, his voice offends me". During a second interview, the interviewer again said, "Your diction, which I can only like to that of a costermonger, will not do for the theatre". However, in 1936, he was accepted as assistant stage manager at the

Connaught and later he played in rep touring the northern towns. In 1939, he left for America and when he stopped off in California, he was offered a part by the Edward and Small studio in the film, 'The Man in the Iron Mask'. This led to other films and, to find the fare to return to England, he also worked as a night porter at the YMCA. He signed on as a deckhand on a ship and arrived back in 1942. He joined ENSA and appeared at the Garrison Theatre where he met an actress, Helen and they married in 1943. After Helen's death in 1971, Peter made 32 films, immersing himself in his work and not socialising. I might also add that Helen will always be remembered as she has a rose named after her.

I have not mentioned his time with Hammer Films as I'm sure we are all familiar with these. We are pleased that he chose Whitstable as his home from 1957 and played a large part in the preservation of Old Whitstable. He was patron of the Images Theatre Company.

Peter Cushing died on 11 August 1994 and we shall most certainly miss him but, as with his wife, we have a permanent memorial - Cushing's view - and the bench donated by him from his garden.

Theatre, Television and Film Credits:

1940-1975	36 theatre appearances
1951-1984	52 TV appearances
1939-1985	90 film appearances

Awards:

1953/54	Outstanding Actor of the Year
1956, 1973	Best Actor
1975	The Licorne d'Or Award for Best Actor (France)

Wynn Ellis - philanthropist - (1790-1875)

Wynn Ellis was born in Oundle in 1790 and at the age of 22 came to London and established himself as a hosier and mercer at Ludgate

Hill. From 1830 until 1871, he was a wholesale silk merchant until his retirement, having made a fortune.

He was Radical MP for Leicester for two terms and advocated the repeal of the Corn Laws, those relating to bankruptcy and the abolition of all import duties. For a year, he was Sheriff of Hertfordshire, disposing of his properties when he became ill. An avid collector of painting, furniture and marbles, on his death he left all of his Old Masters to the National Gallery. Of the 402 offered, only 42 were accepted and the rest of his treasures were auctioned at Christie Manson and Wood, fetching over £5600, a very high price.

His Gainsborough portrait of the Duchess of Devonshire, bought by Thomas Agnew and Sons, fetched the highest price ever paid at a public auction - £10,000. In 1876, it was stolen and a reward of £1000 offered but it was not recovered.

For many years, he lived at Tankerton Towers with his mistress and their children. He refused to become sheriff but he was a JP for Kent and owned the Feakins Mill in Belmont Road.

Mrs Ellis died in 1972 after 58 years of marriage and is buried in All Saints Church in a mausoleum designed by Edward Middleton, son of Sir Charles Barry, architect of the Houses of Parliament. Wynn Ellis died in 1975 at the age of 85 and was buried next to his wife. Most of his fortune was left to religious and charitable organisations.

A lasting memorial to this very generous and charitable gentleman, namely the Alms House in Tower Parade, was built with money left by this Victorian philanthropist. In these houses, there is accommodation for eight single women and four married couples. Single women received 4s a week and married couples 5s a week. £2 in coals yearly. Rent 1d a week.

Trader Horn - (Alfred Aloysius Smith) - adventurer and author - (1861 - 1931)

He was born in Liverpool and ran away to sea in 1870. He went to South Africa and travelled extensively, exploring wild and dangerous places, meeting slave traders and prospecting for gold. He took part in the Jameson raid and fought in the Boer War.

His body scarred through combats with wild animals, he then travelled to America, appearing with Buffalo Bill but he lost contact with his family, only being reunited with them through his books. 'The Waters of Africa', 'The Young Vikings' and 'The Ivory Coast Earlies' were bestsellers and his memoirs by Etherelda Lewes covered three books and sold more than 120,000 copies in America alone. He also made films for Gaumont Pictures and Metro Goldwyn Mayer and on his death these two studios sent wreaths.

He lived in Joy Lane until his death in 1931 in St Helier's Nursing Home. A Roman Catholic, he was buried in Whitstable Cemetery with his three most prized possessions - his stetson hat, a Zulu shield and his old pioneering rifle.

Bertram (Bertie) Lamb - alias Uncle Dick - (1889-1938)

He was born in 1889 and joined the Daily Mirror before the Great War. In 1914 he joined the Middlesex Regiment and was commissioned as war correspondent. On being demobbed, he returned to the Mirror and was invited to edit a children's corner. He hit upon the idea of having a comic strip and invented three characters who became world famous as the Pets - a dog called Pip, a penguin called Squeak and a hare called Wilfred. These three lovable pets had their own club, Wilfred's League of Gugnuncs, which raised money for children's parties. Rallies were held in the Albert Hall and in 1928 no less than 8000 people attended, raising money to provide hospital beds and playgrounds for children.

His efforts were backed by several members of the royal Family and on one occasion, when the Pets and their creators were presented to King George and Queen Mary, Squeak actually bit the Queen.

In 1926, Bertie married Greta Reeves, George Reeves' daughter, and lived in Chestfield, the village created by his father-in-law. There were two daughters, one of whom died in childhood. Greta was later to achieve fame by contributing to women's magazines from 1939 onwards and was for some years the critic for the Fathers and Bystander.

At the height of his fame, Bertie contracted TB which in those days was incurable and he was admitted to a clinic but alas he died in Montreaux in 1938 aged 49.

The Pets continued for some years, still drawn by A B Payne who had joined Bertie at the birth of the Pets but the whole thing now lacked Bertie's inspiration and whimsical personality and the feature was eventually dropped. There are many thousands of people worldwide who remember the Pets and their creator with great affection.

Annuals and other memorabilia are now collectors' items.

There is a memorial plaque to Bertie in All Saints Church and a memorial exhibition was mounted in Whitstable Museum to mark the 50th anniversary of his death.

W Somerset Maughan - author - (1874-1965)

Willie Somerset Maughan came from Paris to live in Whitstable at the age of ten after the death of his father, his mother having died two years previously. He lived with his only relative, an uncle, Rev Henry McDonald who was the vicar of Whitstable and his straightlaced but kindly German wife.

He was devastated when his nurse was sent back to France and was soon to find out the differences in his lifestyle in England from that in France. Because of his uncle's attitude to class, he had few friends and the Sabbath was strictly observed as he was expected to set an example to other children.

To brush up his English, he was tutored at Ivy House in Oxford Street, the home of the Etheridges and was accepted as a boarder in the junior school of King's School Canterbury where he was teased because of his stammer.

He worked hard, became Head Boy and won a scholarship to enter the main school. Mr Field, the headmaster, gave encouragement to this clever but difficult boy but two bouts of pleurisy interrupted his studies to enter Cambridge.

He left King's to study at Heidelberg University in Germany, returning at the age of 18 but he was unsettled, leaving an office job after only a few weeks. He then studied medicine at St Thomas's in London and qualified but did not practise. His experiences in the poor quarters gave him ideas for his book, 'Liza of Lambeth, in 1897.

His uncle, the Rev McDonald, died in 1895 and is buried in All Saints churchyard.

He wrote mainly of his life in Whitstable in 'Of Human Bondage', 'Mrs Craddock' and 'Cakes and Ale', dealing with attempts to break down class barriers. Some characters in 'Cakes and Ale' are thought to defame local residents and he suffered unpopularity on that account. In the book, the name Whitstable was altered to Blackstaple.

He twice visited the town in his seventies and stayed at the Bear and Key Hotel.

He was co-opted to the Board of Governors at Kings, donating his books and many other gifts to the school and, in his eighties, he visited for the opening of the Science Lab which he financed as well as the Maughan Library.

There is little to see now of his life in the town. The Vicarage and Ivy House have been demolished. Lime House in 'Cakes and Ale' was demolished when the Congregational Church was built and is now the Playhouse Theatre. A plaque in the entrance hall donated by the Quill Club and unveiled by his niece is the only memorial to him in the town.

Court Lees, which lies between Whitstable and Canterbury, the Jolly Sailor and the Golden Lion are also mentioned in his book.

Somerset Maughan was 91 when he died in 1965 and his ashes, at his request, are buried in the grounds of King's School within the Cathedral precincts.

Wanda Morgan - golfer

This lady was outstanding in her field, so much so that she was mentioned in the Guinness Book of Records.

I will list her many victories from 1929-1956.

1929	Round of 60 gross on 73 par at Westage
1930, 1931, 1933,)	
1935, 1936, 1937,)	Kent Championship
1953)	
1931-1937, 1953	English International vs Scotland, Ireland and Wales
1932, 1934, 1936	Curtis Cup
1931	British Open Championship, runner-up to Enid Wilson
1932-37	England vs France
1934	England vs Canada
1935	English Open Championship, beating Pam Barton
1941/42	Daily Graphic National Tournament (wartime get-together)
1948	Sunningdale Foursomes with Sam King
1948	Worplesdon Foursomes with Eustace Scorey
1956	Fairway and Hazard Foursomes

For years, Wanda resided in one of the old Golf Cottages until her death in 1997 and enjoyed reminiscing about the Old Whitstable, of which she was very fond.

Fred Pursey - boxer - (1917-   )

Fred was born in Belvedere in 1917, moving to Whitstable in 1923.

He started boxing as an amateur in 1931 aged 13 ½ years while in the Sea Scouts and then for the Sylvan Boxing Club, Nonington and Canterbury Lads Club.

He served in the RAF from 1939-45, first as a PTI and later as a dispatch rider serving in England, France and India.

Between 1937 and 1942 he was managed by Frank Clements of the East Kent Sporting Club and in 1942 by John Hammins of the Dorchester Hotel.

As an amateur from 1931 to 1937, he won 18 bouts. In 1937, he turned professional - 18 wins, 9 lost, 1 draw.

Between 1938 and 1942 he was Kent Featherweight Champion and retired in 1942. He is still the unbeaten featherweight champion and is very proud of his championship belt which he still has.

Fred was tipped by the famous manager Walter Day (Lowestoft) and Ted Broadribb as a certain British champion.

A carpenter by trade, he has now retired.

Jack and Roger Livesey - actors

There is very little documentation on these two gentlemen although they come from a well-known theatrical family, sons of Sam Livesey who was not as famous as Jack and Roger.
Jack lived at the Golf Cottages, often visited by his brother. He starred in various films, including 'The Wandering Jew' and 'Passing of the First Floor Back'. He died in 1961 aged 60.

Roger was more famous than his father and brother. He divided his career between stage and screen and appearances included 'The Old Curiosity Shop', 'Where the Rainbow Ends', 'Cuckoo in the Nest', 'Fourth Parallel' and 35 others. He was recognised for his unmistakable 'gravel voice'. He died in 1976 aged 70.

Frank Ward Smith - journalist

Frank Ward Smith was a well-known BBC war correspondent, having made the first broadcast eye-witness account of the D-Day landings on the beaches of Normandy.

A Fleet Street journalist, he wrote for a number of dailies and was a frequent contributor to the short story section of the old Evening Standard.

He arranged non-denominational visits to the Holy Land. These were so successful that the Roman Catholic church honoured him with the title of custodian of the Holy Land, making him the only non-Catholic to hold this title.

Lawrence Irving - set designer - (died 1990)

Lawrence Irving was the grandson of the famous Shakespearian actor and founder of the Theatre Museum.

His father was an actor and his mother, Dorothea Baird, was a very well-known actress so it is a wonder he did not enter the profession. Instead, he became an artist, stage designer and author. Three of his books, 'The Precarious Crust', 'The Actor and his World' and 'The Successors' were bestsellers. He designed the sets for films such as 'Pygmalion', 'Blithe Spirit', 'The Good companions' and many more. During the war he rejoined the RAF in despatches in France and the Tactical Air Force in Belgium 1943-45 and was awarded the OBE.

The Irvings lived at The Mill at Borstal Hill for a number of years, living in the farmhouse and using the mill as a studio.

Lawrence left Whitstable to live in Wittersham where he died in 1990. Mrs Irving died in 1978. They are survived by a son and a daughter.

NOTORIOUS WHITSTABLE

The Stella Marris Murder

In 1926, Whitstable was all agog over the Stella Marris murder, so named as it was committed at a house of that name in St Anne's Road.

Today it would be called a crime of passion.

It involved three people - Francis (Frank) Smith, his wife, Kathy, who was ten years his junior, and John Durham, Herne Bay's champion rink hockey player. Both men had similar backgrounds. Smith was the grandson of a Canadian millionaire and was a playboy who supposedly squandered a fortune of half a million pounds. Durham was the son of a barrister and both had been educated at Eton and Cambridge.

In January 1926 Mr and Mrs Smith met Durham who was separated from his wife and the three became firm friends. Smith became suspicious that his wife and Durham were having an affair and the men came to blows. In June, Smith left home to go to London sending Kathy, the nanny and children to a cottage which belonged to Durham's father. Smith came to the cottage and sent the children home saying that his intention was to break up the cottage and kill them both. However, Kathy left and rented Stella Marris.

In August, Smith bought a gun and arrived at his wife's home. She allowed him to stay when he told her that he intended to kill himself. She promised not to see Durham again and it seemed that they were reconciled but this was not so as Kathy told him to leave which he refused to do. Smith sent a telegram under Kathy's name asking Durham to come to her. When he came, they sat together in a restaurant with Frank only drinking champagne and Kathy and Durham eating a meal. They all returned to Stella Marris where Kathy prepared a bed for Durham. Smith said that he would not have a lover staying but Kathy laughed and ignored him.
A Mr Barton who was passing by the house noticed three people moving about and, hearing a shot, looked back and saw Durham and Kathy move towards Smith. Durham fell to the ground, was struck by Smith as he fell and died later.

At Maidstone Assizes, his defence was that the shooting was accidental and he hadn't touched the trigger. He was also charged with possessing a firearm with intent to endanger life. Sir Edward Marshall Hall QC made an impassioned speech and the jury found him not guilty but he was sent to prison for one year's hard labour for the firearms offence.

He was divorced after leaving prison and died in November 1944 at Ilfracombe in Devon.

William Joyce

I heard what I then thought was a fairy tale that William Joyce had lived in Tankerton but after reading an article in the Whitstable Times I realised it was fact not fiction.

Born in Ireland, he was a fanatical fascist and disciple of Moseley, whose followers were a treacherous, cruel and ruthless gang of thugs named the Black Shirts although the local members wore brown shirts. Even the uniforms gave one a feeling of foreboding and disgust.

Joyce left England on the evening of 1 September 1939 for Germany to broadcast propaganda from there under the name of Lord Haw Haw - at least, that was the name we knew him by. He started his broadcast "Germany calling, Germany calling", trying to undermine the morale of the British people. At first we tuned into him as he had a wonderful knowledge of the ships that had been sunk and servicemen who had been taken prisoners, quoting their names and service number, even before the next of kin had been notified by our authorities. As time passed he became a butt for wireless and music hall comics and even Winston Churchill joked about him. According to the Whitstable Times, he owned a wireless parts shop opposite the harbour gates and lived at Jocelyn, Herne Bay Road. The house was named after his first wife and his surname.

After the defeat of Germany, he was brought back to England, tried, convicted as a traitor and was hanged in 1944.

Murders in Whitstable

Between the wars there were several murders in Whitstable. I will not name the people as the families are still living in the town and I feel that they have suffered enough. To see it in print would cause them unnecessary distress and I have therefore left some space at the end of this book to note any that you remember if you so wish.

SOME WELL-KNOWN RESIDENTS

Granny Allen

Granny Allen, as everyone knew here, was at the beck and call of all, a short rotund lady, jolly, the kind of person one could talk to.

Her husband was a fisherman and they lived in Middle Wall with their seven children.

In the Twenties and Thirties and probably even before that she attended the birth of many babies, born in the family home, often charging as little as 5/- as alternative care was too expensive for some parents.

Another of her tasks was to 'lay people out'. This meant washing and generally attending to the deceased ready for the undertaker. She used to say, "I see them into the world and see them out of it".

I understand that it was requested that her name should be put forward for recognition from the Palace. It is not know if she received it before she died at the age of 93.

W Pettman - Billy Plum Bun

He was so named as he went around the town selling currant buns - he was a baker by trade.

For such a small man he had a very large head and it was said that after his death it was to be donated for medical research.

Mr Burrows (Duke of Wapping)

Very little is known about this man who was well-educated and, in his more lucid moments, interesting to talk to. Whether he was a victim of the Great War or whether he had had business troubles is not know,

He was tall, dressed in a raincoat and trilby hat and he carried a walking stick.

The youth of the town taunted him by 'blowing raspberries' and shouting at him. This resulted in him shouting back and throwing the stick in the air. I have often wondered if these men now think back and on reflection are shamed of their behaviour to this poor man. I hope so.

Dot Carson (1894-1990)

Born in Willesden, London, she came to live at Borstal Hill at the age of 16 and became a ballerina at Covent Garden. In 1914 she worked as a Red Cross nurse at the Marine Hotel which was used as a hospital and later at the Barn House which was used as a convalescent home for wounded soldiers.

Nurse Carson owned a Daimler, one of the first cars in the town. She was asked to meet a train and she thought she was meeting wounded soldiers but to her surprise it was Queen Mary. She drove her to Barn House, the first woman ever to drive the Queen.

She was a devoted follower of Kent County Cricket Club. She will be sadly missed for her warmth and sense of humour. She died in the St John's nursing home at the age of 96.

Nancy Foreman (1900-1992)

This lady, a cousin of mine, was born in Whitstable in 1900 and until the early Eighties carried on her family's business, driving a taxi as she had done for sixty years.

Her mother, like my mother, was the daughter of Peter Merritt who had the first carrier's business operating from Whitstable to Canterbury. In the early Twenties the passage between the Bear and Key Hotel and Tooleys wine merchants, where he stabled his horses, was named after him. It has since been renamed.

Nancy and her husband, Herbert (Herbie) Ashby, ran Foremans Taxis until his death in 1969.

Nancy had many regular clients, some of whom she ferried from their homes to catch the commuter trains and met them on their return. It was not unusual for her to work from 8.00am until 1.00am

Her memories were many and varied, particularly of the pre-war times when the holiday trade was booming. She had a clean licence which was quite a feat considering the number of years spent behind the wheel in the town she had spent all of her life. She died in November 1992. I am surprised there was not a write-up in the local paper as there had been when she was 70 and still driving the taxi.

Charlie Knowles (1894-1966)

To write a complete dossier on Charlie would take pages and pages to do him justice so unfortunately I will have to condense a summary sent to me by his son, Gordon.

Born in Faversham into a family of fruiterers, it seemed inevitable that he would enter his father's business although his ambition was to become a professional footballer. Falling out with his father, he moved to Dover to the business there.

During the 1914-18 war he joined the Garrison Artillery working with objects called 9-2s. It was reported that a German submarine was in the Channel so Charlie, with others, manned the guns and shelled a dark object on the horizon. Due to his erratic firing he missed it which was lucky because it was not a submarine but a British trawler! He became a batman but he did not enjoy this, particularly the lighting of fires so he used paraffin and almost set fire to the barracks. He became ill and was invalided out.

In 1917 he started up business in Whitstable with his only trouble being bank managers - he went through every bank in the town.

His name has appeared a number of times in the local paper: in 1920 selling bathing cabins for £7 each; in 1934 summoned for not supplying wholesome water to his caravans and ordered to pay £1-3-6d; but the outstanding case was the order to demolish his bungalows at Seasalter stating that they were insanitary. This incensed the family so much that Charlie and his sons began their offensive by interrupting Council meetings and displaying placards from the public seats. The police were called and order was restored but this was only the beginning. One evening a number of us were outside the Castle and were refused entry so Charlie saw the key in the door and turned it, locking the Council inside and to the humiliation of the Council it was reported to the daily newspapers.

At the height of the bungalow affair a man phoned Charlie asking if they were insured and offering to burn them down. He informed the police, demonstrating that at heart he believed in law and order.

He had a terrific sense of humour. In the shop a notice read, "Line your pockets with pigskin so that the pennies come out with a grunt". Another read, "Make your eye the judge, your pocket your guide and money the last thing to part with".

Lorries were to be seen all over Kent bearing the logo, "Clap hands, here comes Charlie". An astute businessman, he would judge orchards assessing the amount of fruit each would produce. I remember walking along the High Street on Saturday evenings in the summer buying fruit from him at a ridiculously low price.

He was also a Town Councillor before the bungalow incident. Needless to say he was very outspoken.

He married in 1913. His two sons, Gordon and Eric, and his

daughter, Hazel, entered the business. For some years they lived at 'Jaffa' - aptly named - in Canterbury Road. This has since been demolished and replaced by flats.

For years he played for the local town cricket club boasting that he had broken more windows in Church Road than any other cricketer. His one ambition to knock a hole in the gasometer was, luckily, not granted. He caused much amusement with spectators not knowing if he was batting or fielding. He was President of the Whitstable and Tankerton Cricket Club until 1959 when he retired, against opposition, due to ill health. In honour of his work and support, the new gateway to the cricket section was named Knowles Gate.

With his passing in December 1966 at the age of 72, Whitstable lost one of its most colourful characters in both the sporting and business fields.

This is a section of a poster printed in 1932:

King Edward potatoes	7lbs 6d	7/- cwt
Majestic white potatoes	4lbs 3d	5/6 cwt
Carrots, Turnips, Onions	7lbs 6d	
Large Jaffa oranges	1d each	
Messina lemons		2 a 1d

Delivered free

John Kemp

John Kemp was the most 'used' undertaker in the town, a distinguished-looking man who performed his duties impeccably and with dignity.

No matter how far the home of the deceased was from the cemetery or churchyard, he walked in front of the hearse at a very steady pace, the six pallbearers at the side.

He was also a builder, his workshops being in Albert Street next to Albert Street Passage.

A staunch Congregationalist, he lived with his wife in Tankerton Road. They had two sons.

Walter Camburn (Skimps)

A lovable tramp, that is until someone upset him, he lived in a hut in Clowes Wood although as children we thought he lived in a small hut at the top of Duncan Down. He was very religious, at times gentle and unassuming but, as I have said, if he was upset he became abusive.

He enjoyed conversing with passers-by and was often seen sitting on a stone at the bottom of Borstal Hill near Carters Nurseries. He relied on the locals to keep him supplied with food and clothing.

Children were discouraged from speaking to him as he was unwashed but he was harmless. On one occasion I asked him why he wore more than one overcoat at a time. The answers was to keep out the cold in the winter and the heat out in the summer.

It is not known if in the past he had been a sailor as he always wore a cheesecutter cap and walked with a large thick stick.

Ismay Trimble

There is not a lot to say about this lady except (I believe) she was the first female councillor to sit on the Council.

She was a large lady often seen cycling or driving her yellow Morris Minor, a small car for such a large person.

Dan Sherring

What can be said about this eccentric, clever, unforgettable and fun-loving man that has not already been said. So many tales have been told about him, some true, others questionable. The one of his pulling the communication cord as he travelled from London for a bet, the conflicting accounts of the coffin he supposedly had made, his sightings of ghosts in Joy Lane, his appearance one Sunday evening at the Cross, dressed as and impersonating a Mormon to a large audience. Knowing him, he was not taken seriously.

Browsing through the old copies of the Whitstable Times at Colindale, there were two snippets that typified him. His Seasalter Carnival I have mentioned in my chapter on 'Seasons'. The second was when he advertised to give lessons and to compete in a boxing bout starting at 7.30pm and finishing soon afterwards.

Although he was a jester, there was a serious side to him. By profession he was an artist, although originally a draper, a dedicated sculptor and painter of many scenes, with the canvas of the Whitstable sunset a masterpiece.

He was commissioned by King George V to do a painting of Sandringham and this now hangs in Buckingham Palace. Two of his paintings were auctioned in aid of the hospital fund.

Henry Skinner (Harry)

He was born in Ramsgate and the family moved to Whitstable in 1890.

From 1904-1914 he sailed in the brigantine, Raymond, which was owned by Billy Dadd and later joined the hospital ship, HMT Minnetonka, until it was torpedoed in 1917. He then joined her sister ship, Miniwaska, and after the war joined the merchant ships, Missouri and Infredean.

In 1912 he married Ida and had three offspring, Sybil, Jean and Peter. Unfortunately Ida died in 1927. Harry remarried and had Pamela and Kenneth.

Whilst waiting for a berth, he worked at Reeves Saw Mills and had an accident losing two fingers and the thumb of his right hand which meant his sailing days were over. He then did various jobs working for the council and navigating for Lawrence Irving on his yacht, the Lady Mary, and in 1926 joined the East Kent Gas Light and Coke Company as the lamplighter. This is now a thing of the past but he will be remembered riding his bicycle with a long pole with a hooked nail at the top in his hand pulling the chain on the lamp to light or put out the flame whilst never dismounting. In 1932 the lamps were fitted with time clocks by Frank Sharp and Freddie Cage but Harry still had to make his rounds to make sure they were functioning and carrying spare mantles on windy nights. During the day he altered the clocks. Looking back I realised the long hours he worked - from 6.30am to 5.30pm - then cycling around Whitstable and Tankerton and at 10.30pm putting out the lamp outside St Alphege Church. He did this seven days a week although he did have Saturday afternoon off and Sunday during the day. The only respite was Christmas Day and his one week's holiday and for this he was paid the princely sum of £2-10s a week.

When hostilities began, a lamplighter was no longer needed and he was transferred to the maintenance workshop. He retired in 1951 and died in 1961.

I have given this account of my father's working life as he will be remembered by so many residents of the town.

Chapter Nine

EDUCATION

In the Twenties and Thirties, the education received in the state elementary schools was very basic but it provided a solid foundation for future use. Great emphasis was put on the three 'Rs' and mental arithmetic in particular was a must for we did not have such aids as calculators. Neatness in writing was also demanded.

Discipline was avidly enforced with offenders being given the cane, rule or a jolly hard smack. I should know - I have been on the receiving end many times! Seldom did parents object, probably as they themselves were strict.

There were no playgroups or pre-school classes.

From ages five to eight, children attended primary school, from eight to fourteen they went to junior and senior school. At the age of 11, pupils sat the 11+, a written test, then another written test at the chosen school. If you passed these, you had the ordeal of the oral exam and if you were one of the lucky few, you entered the grammar school. On completing their education there and providing the results of the entry exams were satisfactory, they were accepted at a university. Again, there were very few places and to pass you had to have a high IQ. Keeping children at these schools was difficult for parents as grants were not easily available.

For those attending the Endowed Girls and the Boys Council schools, apart from history, geography, English and arithmetic lessons, there was wood and metalwork and gardening for the boys and knitting, needlework and housewifery for the girls. Miss Woodhams taught at the cookery school in Albert Street and gave the girls a good training in the art of housewifery.

Organised sport was cricket and football for the boys and netball, tennis, rounders and country dancing for the girls. Looking back, I wonder why there wasn't a swimming pool. I should have thought it essential living in a seaside town.

For those leaving school at 14, there were classes available for a fee in shorthand, typing and book-keeping.

Children living in outlying districts were brought to school by bus - free.

In 1920 there was no school canteen, except for the bus children at a cost of 4d and the poor were given a free meal to "save them falling asleep during lessons". This was supplied by an outside caterer. As we approached the Thirties, meals costing 5d were cooked at the canteen at the boys' school and towards 1939 6d bought meals for local children.

The one thing pupils dreaded hearing after having played truant was a knock on the door by Mr Richards, known as the School Attendance Officer, who wanted to know why you hadn't been to school. In 1925 a father was fined 5/- for not making sure that his child had gone to school.

I visited Westmeads School recently and was impressed by the refurbishment with modern and colourful furniture replacing those heavy wooden desks. The teachers were approachable and there was a happy atmosphere. I remembered as a young child at assembly marching round the hall to the piano playing 'In an English Country Garden'. Apparently they no longer ring the bell in the belfry but I noticed that the picture which used to hang above Miss Powell's desk - a print of Christ surrounded by children of all nations dressed in national costume and with the caption 'Suffer little children to come unto me' - is now missing. This picture impressed me so much that for years I have tried to purchase a similar one but so far without luck. I'll keep on trying.

In 1930 milk was supplied for ½d a day, Horlicks and cod liver oil and malt for 1d.

I had intended to write remarks against each teacher but, as there were conflicting comments from the ex-pupils I have spoken to, I have decided to leave this for you to do.

Westmeads

Miss Powell (headmistress)
Miss Page
Miss Ougham
Miss Porter
Miss Woodman

St Alphege

Miss Carswell (headmistress)
Miss Cook
Miss Cornfoot
Mrs Armstrong

The Endowed School and the Oxford St School were mixed. In 1924 they separated them to make the Endowed School for Girls and the Oxford Street School for Boys.

The Endowed School

Miss Carter (headmistress)
Miss Ougham
Miss Kemp
Miss Foreman
Miss Pay
Miss Campey
Miss Saunders
Miss Bartlett
Miss Pearce
Miss Brightman
Miss Wood
Miss Howell

Miss Abrahams
Miss Woodhams (cookery school)
Mrs Ludlam
Mrs Abrahams

Boys Council School

Mr Palmer (headmaster 1923-27)
Mr Sparshott (headmaster 1927-28)
Mr Wells (temporary headmaster 1928)
Mr Shoesmith (headmaster 1928-31)
Mr Metcalfe (headmaster 1931-35)
Mr Newcome (headmaster 1935-60)
Mr Skidmore
Mr Kemp
Mr Ireland
Mr Laws
Mr Bateson
Mr Sheard
Mr Cunningham
Mr Martin
Mr Parnell
Mrs Pile (kept a box of winter mixture on her desk. Bribery?)
Mr London
Miss Howell
Mr Overton (temporary)

The pupils had their own newspaper called Tach.

Grammar Schools (Boys)

Kent College, Canterbury
Simon Langton, Canterbury
Grammar School, Faversham

Grammar Schools (Girls)

William Gibbs, Faversham
Simon Langton, Canterbury

Private Schools

Mr Saunders, Collegiate School, Shaftesbury Road
Mr Sargeant, Clare House School, Church Street
Miss Stevenson, Dunelm College, Canterbury Road
(later Tankerton Road)
Miss Lamb, Meadowcroft, Church Street
Miss Sonderburg, Nelson Road
Misses Hall and Couldray, St Anne's Road
Miss Sutton, Cromwell Road
Pitman School of Typewriting, Tower Hill

Chapter Ten

STREETS AND OCCUPANTS

VICTORIA STREET

This is a list of the residents of Victoria Street most affected by the mine dropped on 11 October 1941 according to the last street census taken before the war:

1	Nutten S H		**Here is Regent Street**
3	Foreman H		(where the mine dropped)
3a	Boulting	10	Tilley W R - Fried fish shop
7	Harman G	12	Taafs W
9	Tilley H	14	Rigden S S
11	Warner G	16	Walters B
13	Spenceley Miss/s	18	Shingleston E D
15	Maxted F	20	Parker J T
17	Pout Mrs	22	Adams E G
	Here is Bexley Street	24	Collar J
19	Kemp S	26	Stroud J T
21	Parsons Mrs	28	Merritt A J
25	Savage J L - General shop	30	Goatley F W
27	Camburn G	32	Harris E T
29	Hodges P W	34	Wood Miss
31	Warner G		
33	Camburn G		
35	Wraight W		
37	Gummer		
39	Dunn T W		
2	Rowden H		
4	Payne J T		
4a	Fisher T		
6	Harman H - Hairdresser		
6a	Foreman G - Antique dealer		
8	Newman A W		

STREETS AND OCCUPANTS - *Walking from Tollgate to the end of Tankerton Road.*

CANTERBURY ROAD

	1920			1930			1939	
No.	Name	Trade	No.	Name	Trade	No.	Name	Trade
1	Railway Inn	public house	1	unchanged	unchanged	1	unchanged	unchanged
3	House	-	3	Herberts	cycles	3	Anderson	confectioner
3a	House	-	3a	Gisby	confectioner	3a	Gisby	taxi proprietor
5	Emptage	fishmonger	5	unchanged	unchanged	5	Rigden	unchanged
7	Young	wardrobe dealer	7	unchanged	unchanged	7	unchanged	unchanged
9	Pettman	greengrocer	9	unchanged	unchanged	9	unchanged	unchanged
11/15	Houses	-	11/15	unchanged	unchanged	11/15	unchanged	unchanged
17	Rollington	hairdresser	17	unchanged	unchanged	17	unchanged	unchanged
19	House	-	19	Lanham	confectioner	19	Maughan	unchanged
21	Roots	job master	21	Ford & Carter	butchers	21	Carter	unchanged
23	House	-	23	unchanged	-	23	unchanged	-
25	Martin	greengrocer	25	unchanged	unchanged	25	unchanged	unchanged
27/33	Houses	-	27/33	unchanged	-	27/33	unchanged	-
35	House	-	35	unchanged	-	35	Wood	window cleaner
37	House	-	37	unchanged	-	37	unchanged	-
39	George	french polisher	39	House	-	39	unchanged	-

Here is Swanfield Road

	1920			1930			1939	
No.	Name	Trade	No.	Name	Trade	No.	Name	Trade
41	Baker	grocer	41	Robins	unchanged	41	unchanged	unchanged
43	Hayward & Ashcroft	cycle engineer	43	Hayward	unchanged	43	unchanged	unchanged
45	House	-	45	Jackson	post office and stationers	45	Marmont	unchanged

CANTERBURY ROAD (continued)

1920

No.	Name	Trade
51	Ovenden	milliner
53	House	-
55	House	-
57	House	-

1930

No.	Name	Trade
51	unchanged	unchanged
53	unchanged	-
55	unchanged	unchanged
57	unchanged	-

1939

No.	Name	Trade
51	unchanged	unchanged
53	unchanged	-
55	Wallin & Rowe	tobacconists
57	unchanged	-

Here is Harwich Street

1920

No.	Name	Trade
59	Jackson	postoffice, grocer
61/67	Houses	-
69	House	-
71/81	Houses	-
83	Noahs Ark	public house
85/95	Houses	-

1930

No.	Name	Trade
59	Loudwell	grocer
61/67	unchanged	-
69	unchanged	-
71/81	unchanged	-
83	unchanged	unchanged
85/95	unchanged	-

1939

No.	Name	Trade
59	unchanged	unchanged
61/67	unchanged	-
69	Murrell	general store
71/81	unchanged	-
83	unchanged	unchanged
85/95	unchanged	-

Here is Forge Lane

1920

No.	Name	Trade
97	Browning	coal, coke and soda factors
99	Wills	blacksmith

1930

No.	Name	Trade
97	unchanged	unchanged
99	unchanged	unchanged

1939

No.	Name	Trade
97	unchanged	unchanged
99	Browning	upholsterer

Here is Old Kent Cottages, now West End Parade

CANTERBURY ROAD (continued)

	1920			1930			1939	
No.	Name	Trade	No.	Name	Trade	No.	Name	Trade
2	Rogers	boot repairer	2	unchanged	unchanged	2	Vacant	-
3	House	-	3	Bertram	grocer	3	Vacant	-
3a	House	-	3a	Vacant	-	3a	Wilson	nurse
4	House	-	4	Bertram	confectioner	4	Vacant	-
103	Dawson	The Old Vicarage	103	Hayward	greengrocer	103	Vacant	-
2/12	Houses	-	2/12	unchanged	-	2/12	unchanged	-
14	Rigden	garage	14	Maflins	unchanged	14	unchanged	unchanged
16	House	-	16	Maflins	garage	16	unchanged	unchanged
18	House	-	18	Laws	household goods	18	Vacant	-
20	House	-	20	Rainer	ladies' wear	20	Annette	hairdresser
22	House	-	22	Hammond	confectioner	22	Brown	hardware
24	House	-	24	Priestley	fried fish	24	Emptage	unchanged
26	Butcher	dairyman	26	Cottew	unchanged	26	unchanged	unchanged
28	House	-	28	unchanged	unchanged	28	Cook	boot repairer
30	House	-	30	unchanged	-	30	unchanged	-
32	Gann	JP	32	unchanged	unchanged	32	Knowles (Jaffa)	private house

Here is Suffolk Street

	1920			1930			1939	
No.	Name	Trade	No.	Name	Trade	No.	Name	Trade
34	House	-	34	Hicks	tailor	34	unchanged	unchanged

CANTERBURY ROAD (continued)

	1920			1930			1939	
No.	Name	Trade	No.	Name	Trade	No.	Name	Trade
36	House	-	36	unchanged	unchanged	36	Burnetts	apartments
38/44	Houses	-	38/44	unchanged	-	38/44	unchanged	-
46	House	-	46	unchanged	-	46	Bullen	carter
48/54	Houses	-	48/54	unchanged	-	48/54	unchanged	-

Here is Norfolk Street

Here is Norfolk Street

	1920			1930			1939	
No.	Name	Trade	No.	Name	Trade	No.	Name	Trade
56/58	Dawkins	baker	56/58	unchanged	unchanged	56/58	Smith	unchanged
60/70	Houses	-	60/70	unchanged	-	60/70	unchanged	-
72	Two Brewers	public house	72	unchanged	unchanged	72	unchanged	unchanged

Here is Glebe Way

	1920			1930			1939	
No.	Name	Trade	No.	Name	Trade	No.	Name	Trade
76	Granary House	-	76	Saville	doctor	76	Fisher	unchanged
78	house	-	78	unchanged	-	78	unchanged	-
80	Springfield	nursing home	80	unchanged	unchanged	80	unchanged	unchanged

Here is Alexandra Road

CANTERBURY ROAD (continued)

No.	1920 Name	1920 Trade	No.	1930 Name	1930 Trade	No.	1939 Name	1939 Trade
88/90	Houses	-	88/90	unchanged	-	88/90	unchanged	-
92	House	-	92	unchanged	-	92	Sykes	district nurse
94/98	Houses	-	94/98	unchanged	-	94/98	unchanged	-

Here is Joy Lane

Here is Argyle Road

OXFORD STREET

No.	1920 Name	1920 Trade	No.	1930 Name	1930 Trade	No.	1939 Name	1939 Trade
1	Wheeler	confectioner	1	unchanged	unchanged	1	Camburn	unchanged
3	Vacant	-	3	Roylance	musical instruments	3	Petts	grocer
5	Plaisted	stationer	5	Ford	hosier and hatter	5	Pearce	unchanged
	Foresters Hall							
5a	Reeves	builder	5a	Stevens	watchmaker	5a	Hicks	unchanged
7	Reeves Bros	decorators	7	Godfrey	greengrocer	7	unchanged	unchanged
9	Reeves Bros	decorators	9	Cruickshank	grocer	9	Playter	confectioner
11	Willis	fishmonger	11	unchanged	unchanged	11	unchanged	unchanged
13	Beasley	tobacconist	13	Mallion	unchanged	13	unchanged	unchanged
15	House	-	15	Lanes	stationers	15	unchanged	unchanged
17	Rickwood	greengrocer	17	Smedley	unchanged	17	Amos	unchanged
19	House	-	19	unchanged	-	19	Stroud	baker
21	House	-	21	unchanged	-	21	Tustin	watchmaker
23	Etheridge	surgeon	23	Etheridge (Miss)	private house	23	Camburn	tailor
25	Etheridge	house	25	unchanged	unchanged	25	unchanged	unchanged
27	House	-	27	Clay	sewing machines	27	Domestic Company	unchanged

94

OXFORD STREET (continued)

1920

No.	Name	Trade
27a	-	-
29	Huson	grocer
31	House	-
33	Baker	greengrocer
35	WUDC	Council offices
	Council school	boys/girls/infants
37	Coach and Horses	public house
39/41	Co-op	grocers
43	Weatherspoon	boot repairer
43a	-	-
43b	-	-
45	Andrews & Luckhurst	newsagents
47	Gilbert	watchmaker
49	Rogers	greengrocers
51	Wilkinson	boot repairer
53	Camburn	undertaker
55	Oakland	draper

1930

No.	Name	Trade
27a	-	-
29	Bourke and Hays	unchanged
31	unchanged	-
33	Griffey	painter/decorator
35	unchanged	unchanged
	unchanged	boys junior, senior
37	unchanged	unchanged
39/41	unchanged	unchanged
43	Lucille	hairdresser
43a	Churchill	draper
43b	(rear) Harris	baker
45	unchanged	unchanged
47	Cover	cooked meats
49	Sellens	confectioner
51	unchanged	unchanged
53	unchanged	unchanged
55	Hunniset	unchanged

1939

No.	Name	Trade
27a	Austin	hairdresser
29	unchanged	unchanged
31	unchanged	-
33	Rawlins	shoe repairer
35	unchanged	library
	unchanged	unchanged
37	unchanged	unchanged
39/41	Field	furniture dealer
43	unchanged	unchanged
43a	Howell	electrician
43b	unchanged	unchanged
45	unchanged	unchanged
47	unchanged	unchanged
49	Jackson	greengrocer
51	United Footwear	unchanged
53	unchanged	unchanged
55	unchanged	unchanged

Here is Cromwell Road

1920

No.	Name	Trade
57	House	-

1930

No.	Name	Trade
57	Stebbings	dentist

1939

No.	Name	Trade
57	unchanged	unchanged

OXFORD STREET (continued)

1920

No.	Name	Trade
59	Ilderton	doctor's surgery
61	House	-
63	Whichcord	WUDC solicitor
65	Gann	builder
67/69	Howe	grocer
71	Howe	grocer
73	Rigden	motor and cycle works
75/77	Whitmore	baker
	St Alphege School	girls, infants
	-	-

1930

No.	Name	Trade
59	Saville	unchanged
61	Dixon	dentist
63	unchanged	unchanged
65	unchanged	unchanged
67/69	Vyes	unchanged
71	Jarratt	confectioner
73	Court	chemist
75/77	Weatherly	unchanged
	unchanged	infants
	Sports Club	-

1939

No.	Name	Trade
59	Fisher	unchanged
61	unchanged	unchanged
63	unchanged	unchanged
65	unchanged	unchanged
67/69	unchanged	unchanged
71	unchanged	unchanged
73	Gilman & Clarke	unchanged
75/77	Dilnot	unchanged
	unchanged	unchanged
	unchanged	-

Here is Church Road, now Belmont Road

1920

No.	Name	Trade
2	Rowden	bootmaker
4	Wainwright	costumier
6	House	-
8	Wood	Registrar, births and deaths
10	Boulton	taxis
	Parish Hall	
12	House	-
14	House	-
	Oxford Cinema	-

1930

No.	Name	Trade
2	unchanged	secondhand dealer
4	unchanged	unchanged
6	Days	garage
8	unchanged	unchanged
10	Windyridge	hats and gowns
12	Geard	tea rooms
14	unchanged	-
	unchanged	-

1939

No.	Name	Trade
2	Robinson & Rowe	children's clothes
4	Days	garage
6	unchanged	unchanged
8	Revell	hairdresser
10	unchanged	unchanged
12	unchanged	unchanged
14	unchanged	-
	unchanged	-

OXFORD STREET (continued)

1920

No.	Name	Trade
16	Norris	plumber
18	House	-
20	Rigden	motor works
22	House	-
24	House	-
26	House	-
28	House	-
30	House	-
32	Holding	dentist

1930

No.	Name	Trade
16	unchanged	unchanged
18	Perks	house agent
20	Field	house furnisher
22	unchanged	-
24	Hunniset	draper
26	Witney & Barker	doctor's surgery
28	Electricity Company	showrooms
30	Demolished	-
32	Demolished	-

1939

No.	Name	Trade
16	Oxford Cinema	-
18	Oxford Cinema	-
20	Work Box	wool
22	unchanged	-
24	Crawley	grocer
26	Doctors' surgery	six doctors
28	unchanged	unchanged
30	Milner	costumier
32	Frost	dentist

Here is West Cliff and Nelson Road

1920

No.	Name	Trade
34	House	-
36	House	-
38	Amos	builder
40	Cox	LRAM
42	Gibb	milliner
44	House	-
46	Foad	builder
48/54	Houses	-
56	Hillier	watchmaker
58	House	-
60	Kemp	hand laundry
62	House	-

1930

No.	Name	Trade
34	unchanged	-
36	unchanged	-
38	Glynne and Etheridge	doctors' surgery
40	unchanged	unchanged
42	unchanged	unchanged
44	Anderson	coal merchant
46	unchanged	unchanged
48/54	unchanged	-
56	Staddon	unchanged
58	unchanged	-
60	unchanged	unchanged
62	Field	storeroom

1939

No.	Name	Trade
34	Office (?)	?
36	Rigden	builder
38	Glynne	MOH
40	Austin	art needlework
42	Meadon	costumier
44	unchanged	unchanged
46	Private house	-
48/54	unchanged	-
56	Private house	-
58	Co-op	grocery, etc
60	Co-op	grocery, etc
62	Co-op	grocery, etc

OXFORD STREET (continued)

	1920			1930			1939	
No.	Name	Trade	No.	Name	Trade	No.	Name	Trade
64	Court	fishmonger	64	unchanged	unchanged	64	unchanged	unchanged
66	WUDC	Food Office	66	Dobson	Oxford Hotel	66	Marmont	draper
68	Wilks	butcher	68	Tackley & Shead	unchanged	68	unchanged	unchanged

Here is Clifton Road

	1920			1930			1939	
No.	Name	Trade	No.	Name	Trade	No.	Name	Trade
70	Chamberlain	oil and colour	70	unchanged	unchanged	70	unchanged	unchanged
72	East Kent	public house	72	unchanged	unchanged	72	unchanged	unchanged
						72a	Dunk	taxis
74	House	-	74	unchanged	-	74	unchanged	-
76	Bisson	dairyman	76	unchanged	unchanged	76	Barratt	corn and seed
78	Hales	tobacconist	78	Witherspoon	boot repairer			
80	Hollingsworth	oyster store	80	Rigden	corn dealer			

Here is Canterbury Road

High Street

Here is Terry's Lane

OXFORD STREET (continued)

1920

No.	Name	Trade
2	Nicholls	baker
4	Mills	hosiers
6	Westley	chemist
8	Wheeler	oyster rooms
10	Spain	wardrobe dealer
12	Bedford	confectioner
14/16	Lloyds	bank
18	Kemp	stationers
20	Browning	confectioner

1930

No.	Name	Trade
2	unchanged	unchanged
4	Dorea	fancy draper
6	unchanged	unchanged
8	unchanged	unchanged
10	Maxwell Bennett	optician
12	Flinn	dyers and cleaners
14/16	unchanged	unchanged
18	Kemp	toys
20	Hurren	domestic store

1939

No.	Name	Trade
2	Hipperson	unchanged
4	Harris	estate agent
6	unchanged	unchanged
8	unchanged	unchanged
10	Vacant	-
12	unchanged	unchanged
14/16	unchanged	unchanged
18	Siminson	optician
20	unchanged	unchanged

Here is Buss's Alley, changed to Read's Alley

1920

No.	Name	Trade
22	Kirby	upholsterer
24	Penighetti	dining rooms
26	Ainslie	butchers
28/30	Royal Naval Reserve	public house
32	Freeman Hardy & Willis	shoe retailer
34	Wastall	wine merchant
36	Newell	draper
38	Wilks	butcher
40/42	International	grocers

1930

No.	Name	Trade
22	Gas Light & Coke Co	showrooms
24	Wanstall	wine merchant
26	Dewhurst	unchanged
28/30	unchanged	unchanged
32	unchanged	unchanged
34	Newell	draper
36	unchanged	unchanged
36a	Reeves	estate agent
38	Greenstead	unchanged
40/42	unchanged	unchanged

1939

No.	Name	Trade
22	unchanged	unchanged
24	unchanged	unchanged
26	Steward	unchanged
28/30	unchanged	unchanged
32	unchanged	unchanged
34	Woolworths	fancy goods
36	Woolworths	fancy goods
36a	unchanged	unchanged
38	unchanged	unchanged
40/42	unchanged	unchanged

Here is Bonner's Alley

OXFORD STREET (continued)

	1920			1930			1939	
No.	Name	Trade	No.	Name	Trade	No.	Name	Trade
44	Reeves	estate agents	44	unchanged	unchanged	44	Argosy	cinema
46/48	Picture House	cinema	46/48	unchanged	unchanged	467/48	Argosy	unchanged
50	Davey	draper	50	Davey	unchanged	50	unchanged	unchanged
52	Cardwell	milliner	52	Semple	draper	52	unchanged	unchanged
54	Townsend	restaurant	54	Goodwin	unchanged	54	Coats	solicitor
56	Nash	grocer	56	Westminster	unchanged	56	Vyes	unchanged
58	London Westminster Parr	bank	58			58	unchanged	unchanged
60	London Central	butchers	60	unchanged	unchanged	60	Woolley	shoe retailer
62	Watts	fancy draper	62	unchanged	unchanged	62	unchanged	unchanged
64	West	photographer	64	unchanged	unchanged	64	unchanged	unchanged
66	Cooke	tailor	66	West	photographer	66	unchanged	unchanged
68	Scott	dyers and cleaners	68	unchanged	unchanged	68	unchanged	unchanged
70	Worlds Stores	grocers	70	unchanged	unchanged	70	unchanged	unchanged
	GPO	post office		unchanged	unchanged		unchanged	unchanged
72	Smith	baker	72	Chant	toys	72	Boots	chemist
74	Salvation Army	citadel	74	unchanged	unchanged	74	unchanged	unchanged
76	Harding	hairdresser	76	unchanged	unchanged	76	Bartlett and Bisson	dairymen
78/82	Foreman	gents' outfitters	78/82	unchanged	unchanged	78/82	unchanged	unchanged
84/86	Houses	-	84/86	unchanged	-	84/86	unchanged	-
88	Trumble	umbrella maker	88	unchanged	unchanged	88	Clarkson	unchanged

OXFORD STREET (continued)

	1920			1930			1939	
No.	Name	Trade	No.	Name	Trade	No.	Name	Trade
90/92	Houses	-	90/92	unchanged	-	90/92	Gardiner & Allard	solicitors
94	Electric company	offices	94	unchanged	unchanged	94	Windmill	cafe
96	Shaw	art furnisher	96	Vacant	-	96	unchanged	-
98	Rigden	butcher	98	unchanged	unchanged	98	unchanged	unchanged
100/102	Daniels and Collar	fancy repository	100/102	unchanged	unchanged	100/102	unchanged	unchanged
104	Congregational	church	104	unchanged	unchanged	104	unchanged	unchanged
106	Kennett	florist	106	unchanged	unchanged	106	unchanged	unchanged
108	Field	house furnisher	108	Parker	hardware	108	Cribbens	confectioner
110	Hawkins	baker	110	unchanged	unchanged	110	unchanged	unchanged
112	Priestley	hairdresser	112	unchanged	unchanged	112	Tattersall	butcher
114	Cozens	grocer	114	Weatherley	unchanged	114	unchanged	unchanged

Here is Middle Wall, Oxford Street and Bear and Key

HIGH STREET

	1920			1930			1939	
No.	Name	Trade	No.	Name	Trade	No.	Name	Trade
5	Yardley	wine merchants	5	Watts	unchanged	5	Collard and Carling	unchanged
7	Solly	china and glass	7	unchanged	unchanged	7	Gaywood	wireless engineer
9	Hatchard	gents' outfitter	9	unchanged	unchanged	9	unchanged	unchanged
11	Checkfield	tobacconist	11	Ewing	unchanged	11	unchanged	unchanged
13	Prince of Wales	public house	13	unchanged	unchanged	13	unchanged	unchanged

HIGH STREET (continued)

	1920			1930			1939	
No.	Name	Trade	No.	Name	Trade	No.	Name	Trade
15	Reeves	builder	15	unchanged	Chestfield office	15	Knowles	fruiterer
15a	-	-	15a	Reeves	greengrocer	15a	Turner	cafe
17	Wyver & Nicholls	ironmonger	17	Collar	unchanged	17	unchanged	unchanged
19	Home & Colonial	grocers	19	unchanged	unchanged	19	Funnell	butcher
19a	Sells	solicitor	19a	Hills	plumber	19a	unchanged	unchanged
21	Anderson	coal merchant	21	Todd	dressmaker	21	Carpenter	gents' outfitter
23	Rigden	corn merchant	23	Todd	furniture dealer	23	Carpenter	gents' outfitter
25	Fire Brigade Station	-	25	Rigden	corn merchant	25	unchanged	unchanged
27	Racey	confectioner	27	Butler	unchanged	27	Huxtable	unchanged
29	Offredi	restaurant	29	Home and Colonial	grocers	29	unchanged	uchanged
31	Couchman	greengrocer	31	unchanged	unchanged	31	unchanged	unchanged
33	Brett	confectioner	33	unchanged	unchanged	33	Arthur Collar	builders merchant
35	Collar	builders merchant	35	unchanged	unchanged	35	unchanged	unchanged
37	Cox	stationers	37	unchanged	unchanged	37	unchanged	unchanged
39	Knowles	fruiterers	39	unchanged	unchanged	39	unchanged	unchanged
41	Vacant	-	41	Fletcher	butcher	41	unchanged	unchanged
43	Rigden	fishmonger	43	unchanged	unchanged	43	unchanged	unchanged
45	Coleman	oil and colourman	45	unchanged	unchanged	45	unchanged	unchanged
47	Rowden	fishmonger	47	unchanged	unchanged	47	Allen	unchanged
49	Kemp	fruiterer	49	unchanged	unchanged	49	Rudder	greengrocer
51/53	Spenceley	draper	51/53	unchanged	unchanged	51/53	unchanged	unchanged
55	Cotton	hairdresser	55	Woolley	shoe retailer	55	unchanged	unchanged

Here is Youngs Cottages

High Street (continued)

	1920			1930			1939	
No.	Name	Trade	No.	Name	Trade	No.	Name	Trade
57	Hamilton	upholsterer	57/59	Surman	butcher	57/59	unchanged	unchanged
59/61	Surman	butcher	61	Maypole	grocers	61	unchanged	unchanged
63	Hubbard	baker	63	Butcher	unchanged	63	unchanged	unchanged
65	Holden	jeweller	65	unchanged	unchanged	65	unchanged	unchanged
67	Holden	jeweller	67	Barclays	bank	67	unchanged	unchanged

Here is Gladstone Road

	1920			1930			1939	
No.	Name	Trade	No.	Name	Trade	No.	Name	Trade
69	Vacant	-	69	Smiths	baker	69	unchanged	unchanged
71	Spendiff	tobacconist	71	unchanged	unchanged	71	unchanged	unchanged
73	Flower	gents' hairdressers	73	George	unchanged	73	unchanged	unchanged
75	Perks	estate agent	75	Pearks	grocers	75	unchanged	unchanged
77	Holden	baker	77	Lambert	unchanged	77	King	unchanged
79	Rose	jeweller	79	unchanged	unchanged	79	unchanged	unchanged
81	Boatwright	tobacconist	81	Davidge	unchanged	81	Owen	unchanged
83	King	newsagent	83	Webb	unchanged	83	unchanged	unchanged
85	Vacant	-	85	Hunt	footwear	85	unchanged	unchanged
87	Daly	grocer	87	unchanged	unchanged	87	unchanged	unchanged
89	Cardwell	draper	89	Latimer	unchanged	89	unchanged	unchanged
91	Dorman	saddlers	91	unchanged	unchanged	91	unchanged	unchanged

High Street (continued)

	1920			1930			1939	
No.	Name	Trade	No.	Name	Trade	No.	Name	Trade
93	Fisk-More	photographer	93	?	?	93	Tyler	electrician
95	Jackson	tailor	95	Thompson	draper	95	Dixon	fruiterer
97	McMahon	tailor	97	Vacant	-	97	Rowden	hairdresser

Here is St Alphege Church and the Endowed School (rear)

	1920			1930			1939	
No.	Name	Trade	No.	Name	Trade	No.	Name	Trade
99	Theobald	butcher	99	unchanged	unchanged	99	unchanged	unchanged
101	Rowden	hairdresser	101	unchanged	unchanged	101	Vacant	-
	Turner	draper		Meridew	ladies' outfitter		Herbert	cycles
107/109	Wilman	furnishers	107/109	unchanged	unchanged	107/109	Rye	unchanged
111	Ship Centurion	public house	11	unchanged	unchanged	111	unchanged	unchanged

Here is Skinner's Alley

	1920			1930			1939	
No.	Name	Trade	No.	Name	Trade	No.	Name	Trade
113	Skinner	hosier	113	unchanged	unchanged	113	unchanged	unchanged
113a	Griffey	decorator	113a	unchanged	unchanged	113a	unchanged	unchanged
115	Cooper	chemist	115	Cheadle	unchanged	115	unchanged	unchanged

Here is Argyle Road

HARBOUR STREET

	1920			1930			1939	
No.	Name	Trade	No.	Name	Trade	No.	Name	Trade
1	Haikes	draper/milliner	1	Epworth	draper	1	Dawes	restaurant
2	Dawes	cafe and baker	2	unchanged	unchanged	2	unchanged	unchanged
3	Rowden	tobacconist	3	Kennett	confectioner	3	unchanged	unchanged
4	House	-	4	Lawson	cabinet maker	4	Sholl	boot repairer
5	Nicholls	ironmonger	5	unchanged	unchanged	5	unchanged	unchanged
6/7	Houses	-	6/7	unchanged	-	6/7	unchanged	-
8	House	-	8	West	butcher	8	unchanged	unchanged
9	Ford	general shop	9	unchanged	unchanged	9	West	butcher
10	Plymouth Bretheren	gospel hall	10	unchanged	unchanged	10	unchanged	unchanged
11	Shinglestone	hardware	11	unchanged	unchanged	11	unchanged	unchanged
12	House	-	12	Spray	electrician	12	unchanged	unchanged
13	House	-	13	Spray	electrician	13	unchanged	unchanged
14	Fogg	bootmaker	14	Kemp	unchanged	14	Vacant	-
15	Read	wardrobe dealer	15	Worrall	dining rooms	15	unchanged	unchanged
16	Stroud	tobacconist	16	Impett	unchanged	16	Vacant	-
17	Butcher	fruiterer	17	Godfrey	unchanged	17	Vacant	-
18	Poole	watchmaker	18	unchanged	unchanged	18	unchanged	unchanged
19	Paul	tearooms	19	Roberts	confectioner	19	unchanged	unchanged
20/21	Malnicks	London Bazaar	20/21	unchanged	unchanged	20/21	unchanged	unchanged
22	Malnicks	London Bazaar	22	Kemp	builder	22	unchanged	unchanged

Here is Leggett's Lane

	1920			1930			1939	
No.	Name	Trade	No.	Name	Trade	No.	Name	Trade
23	Rye	house furnishers	23	unchanged	unchanged	23	Impett	confectioner

Harbour Street (continued)

	1920			1930			1939	
No.	Name	Trade	No.	Name	Trade	No.	Name	Trade
24	Reeves	optician	24	Reeves	photography	24	Vacant	-
25	Goffin	drapers	25	Davey	house furnishers	25	Vacant	-
26	Pollock	outfitter	26	unchanged	unchanged	26	Vacant	-
27	Pollock	outfitter	27	Camburn	tailor	27	Eldridge	hairdresser
			27a	Kemp	undertaker	27a	unchanged	unchanged
28	Fenner	hairdresser	28	Reeves	tobacconist	28	British Empire	dyers and cleaners
			28a	Reeves	ham and beef	28a	Hadler	butcher
29	Reeves	confectioner	29	Reeves	tearooms	29	unchanged	unchanged
30	Gambrell	confectioner	30	unchanged	unchanged	30	unchanged	unchanged

Here is Red Lion Lane

	1920			1930			1939	
No.	Name	Trade	No.	Name	Trade	No.	Name	Trade
31	Chinnick	confectioner	31	Jeanette	dressmaker	31	Cyco-Radio	wireless, cycles
32	Edmondson	chemist	32	Court	unchanged	32	Gilman & Clarke	unchanged
	Duke of Cumberland							
	Bear and Key Hotel							
33	Humphrey	leather seller	33	unchanged	unchanged	33	Camburn	hairdresser
34	Poyer	oyster merchant	34	Vye & Son	grocer	34	unchanged	unchanged
35	Vye & Son	grocer	35	unchanged	unchanged	35	unchanged	unchanged

Harbour Street (continued)

	1920			1930			1939	
No.	Name	Trade	No.	Name	Trade	No.	Name	Trade
36	Ridout	post office and stationer	36	unchanged	stationer	36	unchanged	unchanged
37	Hippodrome	theatre	37	Palais de Luxe	cinema	37	Davey	house furnishers
						38	Davey	house furnishers

Here is Victoria Street

	1920			1930			1939	
No.	Name	Trade	No.	Name	Trade	No.	Name	Trade
39/40	Blaxland	greengrocer	39/40	unchanged	unchanged	39/40	unchanged	unchanged
41	Allen	butcher	41	unchanged	unchanged	41	unchanged	unchanged
42	Blaxland	fishmonger	42	unchanged	unchanged	42	unchanged	unchanged
43	Foad	furniture dealer	43	unchanged	unchanged	43	unchanged	unchanged
44	Jackson	book dealer	44	unchanged	fruiterer	44	unchanged	unchanged
45	Foad	pram hire and cycles	45	unchanged	unchanged	45	unchanged	unchanged
46	Dadd	boot repairs	46	unchanged	unchanged	46	unchanged	unchanged
47	Waters	art needlework	47	unchanged	unchanged	47	unchanged	unchanged

Here is Albert Street

	1920			1930			1939	
No.	Name	Trade	No.	Name	Trade	No.	Name	Trade
48	Vaughan	antique dealer	48	unchanged	unchanged	48	Bowrey	unchanged

Harbour Street (continued)

		1920		1930			1939	
No.	Name	Trade	No.	Name	Trade	No.	Name	Trade
49	Nelson Inn	public house	49	unchanged	unchanged	49	unchanged	unchanged
50/52	Houses	-	50/52	unchanged	unchanged	50/52	unchanged	-
53/54	Olney	butcher	53/54	Johnson	unchanged	53/54	unchanged	unchanged
55	House	-	55	unchanged	-	55	Simpson	apartments
56/58	Houses	-	56/58	unchanged	-	56/58	unchanged	-

Here is Sydenham Street

		1920		1930			1939	
No.	Name	Trade	No.	Name	Trade	No.	Name	Trade
59	Spray	electrician	59	Creameries	dairymen	59	unchanged	unchanged
60	Woolley	fruiterers	60	Stephens	general shop	60	unchanged	unchanged
61	House	-	61	unchanged	-	61	unchanged	-
62	House	-	62	Herberts	cycle dealers	62	Vacant	-
63	Back	shoe repairer	63	Sholl	unchanged	63	unchanged	unchanged
63a	Wood	monumental mason	63a	Kennett	confectionery	63a	unchanged	unchanged
64	Rowden	fishmonger	64	Emptage	unchanged	64	Napper	unchanged
65	Lawson	grocer	65	unchanged	unchanged	65	Vacant	-
66	House	-	66	unchanged	-	66	unchanged	-
67	Railway Tavern	public house	67	unchanged	unchanged	67	unchanged	unchanged
68	House	-	68	George	hairdresser	68	Parfitt	unchanged
69	House	-	69	Griffin	confectioner	69	unchanged	unchanged

Here is Harbour Place

TOWER PARADE

Tankerton Terrace

1920			1930			1939		
No.	Name	Trade	No.	Name	Trade	No.	Name	Trade
1a	Markwell	estate agent	1a	unchanged	unchanged	1	Glover	amusements
2	Ferneley	confectioner	2	unchanged	post office, confectioner	1a	Wood	greengrocer
3	Foreman	job master	3	Burt	estate agent	2	unchanged	unchanged
4	House	-	4	Burton & Brooks	solicitors	3	Bushnell	wireless engineer
			4	Brooks	vaccination officer Registrar, births and deaths	4	unchanged	unchanged
						4	unchanged	unchanged
			(These renumbered)					
			5	Terry	butcher	5	Sinden	unchanged
			5a	Hamilton	chemist	5a	Stafford	unchanged
			5b	Bolton	stationer	5b	unchanged	unchanged
7	Capon	china warehouse	5c	Bolton	haridresser	5c	unchanged	unchanged
6	Child	greengrocer	6	Vacant	-	6	hopson	estate agent
5	Wells & Evans	fancy repository	7	unchanged	unchanged	7	unchanged	unchanged
4	Kemp	fancy drapers	8	unchanged	unchanged	8	unchanged	unchanged
3	Kemp	estate office	9	unchanged	unchanged	9	unchanged	unchanged
2	Reeve	dairyman	10	unchanged	unchanged	10	unchanged	unchanged
1	Haslett	grocer	11	Cullens	unchanged	11	unchanged	unchanged

Opposite The Alms Houses

Here is Tower Hill and Northwood Road

TANKERTON BEACH

	1920			1930			1939	
No.	Name	Trade	No.	Name	Trade	No.	Name	Trade
	Dadd	bathers' outfitter		Sumpster	fruiterer		Jacques & Watt	amusement arcade
	Chinnick	refreshments		Dadd	bathers' outfitter		Jacques & Watt	amusement arcade
	Jacques	tearooms		Jacques	arcade, fancy goods		Jacques & Watt	amusement arcade
	Malnick	bazaar		Chinnick	bazaar		unchanged	unchanged
	Browning	confectioner		Stroud	tearooms		Rigden	unchanged
	Holmes	restaurant		unchanged	unchanged		Vacant	-
	Terry	refreshment rooms		Butcher	unchanged		unchanged	unchanged
	Halton	refreshment rooms		Acott	unchanged		Vacant	-
	Goldsmith	bathing machines		Sumpster	unchanged		Vacant	-

Opposite

	1920			1930			1939	
No.	Name	Trade	No.	Name	Trade	No.	Name	Trade
				Dadd	bazaar		unchanged	unchanged
				Hopkins	Savoy Restaurant		unchanged	unchanged
				?	souvenirs		unchanged	unchanged
				?	rock and photographs		unchanged	unchanged
	Griggs	tearooms		unchanged	unchanged		Burlton	amusements

Here is Beach Road

Opposite (continued)

	1920			1930			1939	
No.	Name	Trade	No.	Name	Trade	No.	Name	Trade
	Offredi	Marine Restaurant		unchanged	unchanged		unchanged	unchanged
	House	-		unchanged	-		Offredi	Continental Hotel

Reeves Tea Gardens

TANKERTON ROAD

	1920			1930			1939	
No.	Name	Trade	No.	Name	Trade	No.	Name	Trade
2/4	Greatrex	baker	2/4	Goddard	unchanged	2/4	Pickard	unchanged
6	House	-	6	unchanged	unchanged	6	unchanged	unchanged
8	Etheridge	doctor/ Admiralty surgeon	8	unchanged	unchanged	8	unchanged	unchanged
	Carlton Terrace							
9/18	Houses	-	12/28	renumbered	unchanged	12/28	unchanged	unchanged
			30/32	Ilderton & Harris	-	30/32	unchanged	unchanged
			34	House	doctors' surgery	34	House	-
			44	House	-	44	unchanged	-

Here is Tower Road and Church Street Road

TANKERTON ROAD (continued)

	1920			1930			1939	
No.	Name	Trade	No.	Name	Trade	No.	Name	Trade
			46	Frost	dentist	46	unchanged	unchanged
			48	Byers	boys' school	48	Stephenson	Dunelm College

Here is Kingsdown Road

	1920			1930			1939	
No.	Name	Trade	No.	Name	Trade	No.	Name	Trade
			52/90	Houses	-	52/90	unchanged	-
			92	Reeves	estate agent	92	House	-
						94	Mole	chiropodist
						100	Doris Firth	ladies' outfitter

Here is Tankerton Circus, Kingsdown Park and St Anne's Road

According to records available for 1920, Tankerton Road commenced at Ludgate Hill, incorporating Tower Parade which I have listed separately.
From the beginning of Tankerton Road (as it is known today) to Tankerton Circus, only 21 un-numbered houses existed on the left hand side and seven on the right hand side.

TANKERTON ROAD (continued)

	1920			1930			1939	
No.	Name	Trade	No.	Name	Trade	No.	Name	Trade
Not numbered				Burt	estate agent	102	unchanged	unchanged
				Watts	wines and spirits	104	Collard & Carling	unchanged

TANKERTON ROAD (continued)

	1920			1930			1939	
No.	Name	Trade	No.	Name	Trade	No.	Name	Trade
				Seath	wireless engineer	108	Dewhurst	butcher
nos changed during 20s						110	Hawkins	estate agent
						112	Keeble	grocer
				Allen	newsagent	114	Graves	unchanged
						116	Clement Clarke	optician
				Strangsmith	greengrocer	118	Turners	cafe
				Wilkinsons	shoe repairer	120	United Footwear	unchanged
				Robinson	post office, stationer	124	Steele	unchanged
				Fitt	secondhand car pound			

Here is Fitzroy Road

	1920			1930			1939	
No.	Name	Trade	No.	Name	Trade	No.	Name	Trade
			86	Barclays	bank	128	Strangsmiths	greengrocer
			88	Westminster	bank	130	unchanged	unchanged
			90	Cecil Modes	milliner	132	unchanged	unchanged
			92	Fox	linens	134	Vacant	-
						136	Cadle	estate agent
						138	Wainwright	ladies' outfitter
						140	Trant	fishmonger
						142	Couchman	fruiterer
						144	Bartlett & Bisson	dairyman

Here is Baddlesmere Road

TANKERTON ROAD (continued)

	1920			1930			1939	
No.	Name	Trade	No.	Name	Trade	No.	Name	Trade
						146	Hodgeman	fabrics
						148	Elizabeth	hairdresser
						150	Vacant	-
						152	Butcher	baker
						154	Surmans	butcher
						156	Ida Watkins	costumier
				House	-	158	House	-
				Tooleys	bottling company	160	unchanged	-
						162	Tooley	fancy goods

Here is Graystone Road

	1920			1930			1939	
No.	Name	Trade	No.	Name	Trade	No.	Name	Trade
						164	Spicer	health foods
						166	Kemp	builder
						168	Thomas	antiques
						170	Gaywood	wireless engineer
				Houses	-	172	Howard	domestic store
							unchanged	-

Here is Manor Road

TANKERTON ROAD (continued)

	1920			1930			1939	
No.	Name	Trade	No.	Name	Trade	No.	Name	Trade
						184	House	-
						188	Garton	confectioner
				Lillian	costumier	190	Halls	unchanged

Here is Wynn Road

	1920			1930			1939	
No.	Name	Trade	No.	Name	Trade	No.	Name	Trade
				House	-	192	Thorpe Pearson	dealer
						194	unchanged	-
				Eastern Parade		196	Breading & Lilly	hairdresser
			2	Tasker	confectioner	198	unchanged	unchanged
			3	Trafford	cafe	200	Good Companions	unchanged
				Needham	confectionery	106	Wakely	unchanged

Here is Pier Avenue

	1920			1930			1939	
No.	Name	Trade	No.	Name	Trade	No.	Name	Trade
				Webb	tailor	210	Collard & Carling	wines and spirits
						220	Griffiths	ladies' outfitters
				Darwood	outfitter	222	Smythe	unchanged

Here is Ellis Road

TANKERTON ROAD (continued)

1920			1930			1939		
No.	Name	Trade	No.	Name	Trade	No.	Name	Trade
				Wicks	electrician	224	Vacant	-
				Pearson & Howes	estate agents	226	Darwood	gents' outfitters
				Slope	grocer	242	Jenkins	unchanged
				Riordan	newsagents	244	Hedges	unchanged
						246	Rogers & Parkhouse	wools

Here is Herne Bay Road

1920			1930			1939		
No.	Name	Trade	No.	Name	Trade	No.	Name	Trade
			3/17	Houses	-	3/17	Houses	-
			19	Red Gables	hotel	19	Margaret Rosemary	holiday home
			21/31	Houses	-	21/31	unchanged	-
			33	Betty Rawson	home	33	Putney Children's Home	

Here is Kingsdown Road (now Kingsdown Park)

	1920			1930			1939	
No.	Name	Trade	No.	Name	Trade	No.	Name	Trade
			37	Baverstock	Holy Cross Home	37	Castleton	holiday home
			41/57	Houses	-	41/57	unchanged	-

Here is Cliff Road

	1920			1930			1939	
No.	Name	Trade	No.	Name	Trade	No.	Name	Trade
			59/67	Houses	-	59/67	unchanged	-
			69	Mitchell & Camp	board residence	69	Post & Bradley	dental surgeons
			71/77	Houses	-	71/77	unchanged	-
			79	Tophill	grocer	79	unchanged	unchanged
			81	Wood	butcher	81	unchanged	unchanged
			83	House	-	83	Emmerson	grocer

Here is St Anne's Road and Tankerton Circus

Here is St Anne's Road and Tankerton Circus

TANKERTON ROAD (continued)

1920			1930			1939		
No.	Name	Trade	No.	Name	Trade	No.	Name	Trade
				Buckner	chemist	85	unchanged	unchanged
						85a	Standing	hairdresser
				Thomsett	draper	87	Burden	shoe repairer
				Phillips	furnishers	89	Bow Window	cafe
						91	Brown	watchmaker
						93	Burt	estate agent
						95/97	Thomsett	art needlework
						99	Barnes	chemist
						99a	Faulkner	hairdresser
				Lanes	booksellers	101	Gray	unchanged
				Turner	cafe	103	unchanged	unchanged
				Coasts	hairdresser	105	unchanged	unchanged
				Fitt	garage	107	unchanged	unchanged
				Butler	draper	109	Ellis	unchanged
				Keele	music lounge	111	Express	dyers and cleaners
				Emery	tobacconist	113	Sayer	unchanged
				Lane	domestic store	115	Whiting	unchanged
				Lloyds	bank	117	unchanged	unchanged
				House	-	119	Tasker	fruiterer
				House	-	121	Gas and Coke Company	showrooms
				House	-	123	Fitt	bird fancier
						125	Griffin	confectioner
						133	British Valet	dyers and cleaners
						135	Midland	bank

TANKERTON ROAD (continued)

	1920			1930			1939	
No.	Name	Trade	No.	Name	Trade	No.	Name	Trade
						137	Tankerton Hall	Christian Science
							Houses	-

Here is Graystone Road

	1920			1930			1939	
No.	Name	Trade	No.	Name	Trade	No.	Name	Trade
						157	House	-
						159	Gay Adventure	restaurant
				Houses	-	161/165	unchanged	-
						167	Pryor	home-made cakes

Here is Pier Avenue

	1920			1930			1939	
No.	Name	Trade	No.	Name	Trade	No.	Name	Trade
				Reeves	pharmacy	203	Buckner	drugs company
				House	-	207	Newman	fried and wet fish
				House	-	209	Jago	fruiterer
				House	-	211	Blakelock	furniture dealer
						213	Dence	plumber

TANKERTON ROAD (continued)

1920			1930			1939		
No.	Name	Trade	No.	Name	Trade	No.	Name	Trade
						215/217	Houses	-
						239	Pawsey	hairdresser
						239a	Sullivan	sign writers
						241	Hunt	estate agent

SECTION THREE

Life between the Wars

Chapter Eleven

COMPARISONS AND MEMORIES

This morning when I awoke I decided to compare an average day's work and the equipment used with that of my contemporaries in the twenties into the early thirties.

The house is warm due to central heating; I can have a bath or shower as there is ample hot water; I cook breakfast on an electric stove, toasting bread under the grill; and the welcome cuppa is made from water boiled in the electric kettle. I wash up using washing up liquid or placing the dishes in the dishwasher.

I put the laundry into the washing machine, take it out after an hour, almost dry and, if it is needed urgently, I pop it into the tumble dryer.

Making the bed is easy. All it entails is smoothing the bottom sheet and shaking up the duvet.

I vacuum the carpets. Dusting isn't necessary every day.

I have my main meal in the evening so all I need at midday is a snack.

I then tackle the ironing of items that need it using a steam iron that is thermostatically controlled and place the clothes on the radiator to air.

The evening meal is no hassle. I cook dinner on the electric stove or in the microwave, perhaps using a food processor in the preparation.

I can buy food in advance thanks to the freezer and refrigerator - no more sour milk or rancid food.

So, now for a relaxing evening watching television or a video, listening to the radio or a CD or, for the more ambitious, attending an adult evening class.

No matter what job you tackle, it is far less arduous than it was in the twenties and thirties whether it's housework, decorating or even gardening.

****

You must realise that everything was at a standstill until the kitchener was functioning and that did not happen until the ashes were cleared and the top blackleaded. It was then lit using paper and sticks of wood or a gas poker. Providing it behaved itself, there was a blazing fire in about thirty minutes and you did not forget to regulate the damper otherwise a red hot funnel and a chimney fire was the result.

Kettles and saucepans were filled to heat the water for washing and the first cup of tea. We cooked breakfast - we ate a full breakfast then - with bread toasted on a long fork in front of the fire.

We washed up using scraps of soap in a mesh soap-saver for a lather.

Next, bed-making. Feather mattresses were shaken to remove the lumps, sheets and blankets replaced and chamber pot emptied (most washed in the kitchen).

Back downstairs, fill the coal buckets, sweep the floor, shake the rugs, hearthstone the hearth and front doorstep, keep the fire stoked to cook dinner and to heat the room, clean and fill the oil lamps (in the 20s). Looking back, we seemed to have more meals then!

Fridges and freezers were appliances of the future which meant that shopping was done on a daily basis.

Having washed up and done various chores, it was then time to prepare tea, clear up again and settle down until supper time. The men went off to their local or for a stroll to the town, and the women sat knitting or sewing and then it was off to bed to a cold bedroom lit by a candle or nightlight. Sounds primitive, doesn't it but not having known anything different we considered it quite normal.

To have a bath was quite a performance. The large zinc hip bath was placed in front of the kitchener and filled with water from every available pot heated on top of the stove. I remember sitting in the bath with my front roasting, my back cold from draughts and using Sunlight or carbolic soap. The fun began when we had to empty the bath by manoeuvring it through the door to dispose of the contents. However, in the late 20s, there were improvements for some new houses had bathrooms with gas geysers installed over the bath. These were crude and often temperamental objects which dropped verdigris into a tray at the base.

Daily chores became much easier as gas and electricity was put into the older houses enabling folk to indulge in labour-saving apparatus such a lighting, cookers, iron, water heaters, fires, boilers and vacuums and, for entertainment, wireless, radiograms and in 1936 television.

The gas and electric supply was paid for by inserting one penny pieces into a meter which was emptied by a collector.

Looking back, it is no wonder that women looked old at 40. Their days started around 6am and ended about 10pm.

I have not mentioned the washday ritual, and ritual it certainly was.

Saturday   - change bed linen.

Sunday   - put it into soak with soda added to the water.

Monday	- we lit the copper with wood and coal having filled it manually with water. Soap powder was added (Omo or Hudsons and later Persil, Oxydol or Rinso) and brought to the boil. The fire was periodically stoked. The washing was taken out, put through the mangle, rinsed in water to which Reckitts blue bag had been added, and mangled again. Items to be starched were immersed in a solution of common starch or Robins starch which was made in the same way as custard (but using water, not milk!) and then hung on the line with us praying that the weather would be kind and that soot flicks from the chimneys didn't settle on them. If it should rain, the laundry was draped around the room at night or on an overhead airer which was pulley operated.

Hand washing was done in a zinc bath, rubbed up and down on a washing board using Sunlight or Yellow Windsor soap. Soap was bought weeks in advance to harden. |
| Tuesday | - ironing. The irons were heated on the top of the kitchener and they were cleaned each time by rubbing them in a box of silver sand. We tried hard not to scorch the clothes. Another iron used was the gaffering iron for frills or edgings. |
| Wednesday | - airing. The washing was aired round the fire over the fireguard and the wooden clothes horse. One of the most frustrating things was that it seemed that any soot flicks would land on the collar or front of a white garment. |

COST OF FOOD AND OTHER ITEMS

Prices did not change much at all from the 20s until the mid-30s when they became a wee bit cheaper. Here are some typical examples:

Potatoes	1d per lb
Peas	4d per gallon
Tomatoes	2d per lb
Lettuce	2d each
Plums	4d per lb
Cherries	4d per lb
Milk	2d per pint
Sugar	$4\frac{1}{2}$d per 2 lb
Tea	5d-$8\frac{1}{2}$d per $\frac{1}{4}$lb
Cheddar Cheese	10d per lb
Red Canadian Cheddar	11d per lb
Bacon	1/2d per lb
Butter	11d per lb
Eggs	11d per dozen
Bread	$2\frac{1}{2}$d small; $4\frac{1}{2}$d large
Flour	$7\frac{1}{2}$d for 3lb
Custard powder	$7\frac{1}{2}$d per tin (three flavours: standard, vanilla, almond)
Biscuits	$\frac{1}{2}$d per lb (average): 4d for broken biscuits
Jam and marmalade	$7\frac{1}{2}$d for 1lb; $11\frac{1}{2}$d for 2lb
Red salmon	$7\frac{1}{2}$d for small tin; $11\frac{1}{2}$d for large tin
Breakfast cereals	$4\frac{1}{2}$d per packet
Bisto	$2\frac{1}{2}$d and $7\frac{1}{2}$d per packet
Rice	6d and 8d per lb
Pulses	4d per lb
Cooking salt	2d block
Sunlight soap	$4\frac{1}{2}$d for double block
Soda	2d for 2lb
Washing powder	$3\frac{1}{2}$d and 6d per packet

Beer		Half pint: 1½d in 1920; 3½d in 1939
Spirits		8½d single
Wine		2/6d bottle
Crisps		2d per packet
Oysters		5/- per dozen

Other Items

Clothes

Men	Suits	39/6d
	Caps	1/6d - 3/6d
	Boots	9/11d
	Trousers	Flannel 5/11d per pair; Worsted 8/11d per pair
	Shirts	3/11d - 9/11d
Ladies	Coats	2 guineas
	Hats	3/11d - 9/11d
	Shoes	4/11d - 10/11d
	Dresses	4/11d - 8/11d
General	Coal	45/- per ton; 2/4d per cwt
	Paraffin	8d per gallon
	Cycles	£6 in the 20s; £4 in the 30s
	Inner tubes	2/6d
	Bedroom Suite	10 guineas; Bed £5
	Dining Room suite	£15
	Lino	1/11d per sq yd
	Carpet square	£4.19.11d
	Prams	Marmet £7; Pedigree etc £3.10.0 (average); folding 15/6d

Houses	£395 - £495: deposit £25; repayment £1 per week
Land	£1 - £2 per sq ft to be paid by instalments
Rent	8/- - 11/- per week

The prices quoted above are in the price bracket for the average household. Many household appliances such as fires, cookers, irons, typewriters, could be hired for a few pence a week.

CIGARETTES AND TOBACCO

20 cigarettes - 1/-   10 cigarettes - 6d

        Gold Flake
        Army Club
        Du Maurier (ivory or cork tipped)
        Black Cat
        Batchelors
        Senior Service
        Park Drive
        Kensitas
        Capstan
        Ardath
        Craven A

        Players   20 for 11½d

10 cigarettes - 4d   5 cigarettes - 2d

    Woodbines
    Weights
    Club
    Flag
    De Reszke minors (plain cork and ivory tipped)

    Churchmans   10 for 7d   20 for 1/2d

    Various makes of Turkish 10 for 6d

    SOS 1d each

The majority of cigarettes were plain, not cork tipped.

Tobacco   11½d per oz

    St Julian Virginian or Empire
    Players Navy Cut
    Players Virginian
    Players Flake
    Tom Long
    Rodian refills

    8d per oz

    Erinmore Flake
    Erinmore Cigarette

    4½d per ½oz

    Hearts of Oak

Rizla papers - 1d per packet

NEWSPAPERS

1920	1930	1939

Daily

1920	1930	1939
Sketch	Sketch	Sketch
Mirror	Mirror	Mirror
Chronicle	Chronicle	
Express	Express	Express
Herald	Herald	Herald
Mail	Mail	Mail
News		
Telegraph	Telegraph	Telegraph
Financial Times	Financial Times	Financial Times
The Times	The Times	The Times
Sporting Life	Sporting Life	Sporting Life

Weekly

1920	1930	1939
Whitstable Times	Whitstable Times	Whitstable Times
Gazette		
Kentish Observer		
Kentish Gazette		
		Advertiser

Periodicals

1920	1930	1939
John Bull	John Bull	John Bull
Passing Show	Passing Show	
New Statesman	New Statesman	New Statesman
Picturegoer	Picturegoer	Picturegoer
Punch	Punch	Punch
Tatler	Tatler	Tatler
Tit Bits	Tit Bits	Titbits
Illst'd London News	Illst'dLondon News	Illst'dLondon News
	Spectator	Spectator

1920	1930	1939
Periodicals (continued)		
Radio Times	Radio Times	
	Lancet	Lancet
	Lady	Lady
	Answers	
		Picture Post
		Daltons
		Practical Needlework

Magazines

1920	1930	1939
	Home Notes	Home Notes
	Home Chat	Home Chat
	Womans Weekly	Womans Weekly
Wife and Home	Wife and Home	Wife and Home
Eves	Weldons	Pegs Paper
Every Woman	Modern Woman	Ladies Journal
Womans Journal	Womens Pictorial	Ideal Home
Womens Companion	Films Weekly	Red Letter
Womens Illustrated		True Confessions

Comics

1920	1930	1939
Boys Own	Boys Own	Boys Own
Girls Own	Girls Own	Girls OWn
Rainbow	Rainbow	Rainbow
Chatterbox	Chatterbox	Chatterbox
Comic Cuts	Comic Cuts	Comic Cuts
Picture Friend	Chicks Own	Chicks Own
Childrens Own	Tiger Tim	Tiger Tim
Childrens Friend	Butterfly	Butterfly
Girls Weekly	Crackers	Crackers
	Film Fun	Film Fun
	Joker	Joker

1920	1930	1939
	Comics (continued)	
	Wonder	Wonder
	Jester	Chips
	BoPeep	Puck
	School Girl Weekly	Modern Boy
		Dandy
		Beano
		Radio Fun
		Rover
		School Boys Library
		Friends Library

SERVICES

	1920	1930	1939
Gas	1000 cubic feet 4/-	1000 cubic feet 3/6d	1/- per therm
Electricity	KWH 6d	KWH 2d (approx)	KWH 1d
Rates (including water & sewage)	4/6d in the £	11/- in the £	13/2d in the £
Income Tax	6/- in the £	4/- in the £	7/- in the £
Bank Rate	7%	4½% - 3%	4% - 2%
Parcels	2lb - 9d	3lb - 6d	3lb - 7d
Letters	2d for 2oz + ½d each additional 2oz	1½d for 2 oz + ½d each additional 2oz	2½d for 2oz + ½d each additional 1oz
Telegrams (inland)	12 words for 1/- additional words ½d	9 words for 6d additional words ½d	9 words for 9d additional words ½d
(foreign)	2½d a word	unchanged	unchanged
(greetings)		9 words for 6d additional words 1d	unchanged
Telephone (installation charge)	nil	15/- (1934)	26/-
(quarterly charge)	nil	£1	unchanged
(local calls)	3 mins - 2d	3 mins - 3d 50x1d units free	3 mins - 3d
Number of Subscribers*	138 (1922)	416	847

	1920	1930	1939
Wireless licence	10/-	unchanged	unchanged
Car licence	£6 (6hp)	£4.10s (1935)	£7.10s (1940)
Widow's pension	10/- per week	unchanged	unchanged
Dependants	5/- first child 3/- others	unchanged	unchanged
Old age pension	10/- per week	unchanged	unchanged
Population*	9,842	11,201	15,500 (estimated 1937)

* These figures are specific to Whitstable. Everything else applied nationally.

Parcels	Size limit - 3½ft the greatest length Length and girth combined no more than 6ft
Letters	Maximum size - 2ft x 2ft x 1ft
Telegrams	Surcharge for weekend, night and holiday deliveries Priority introduced
Greetings telegrams	were introduced in 1935 and printed on a decorative form in a gold presentation envelope. The address was charged as an extra.
Wireless and TV licence	TV licences were not introduced until June 1946. A joint TV and wireless licence cost £1 a year
Widows and dependants compulsory insurance	This was introduced in 1925, was effective from January 1926 and remained the same until 1946
Legal Aid	Not as we know it today but there were schemes to help the poor. The Poor People's Act was introduced in 1914 for persons showing they had a reasonable case. In 1925 responsibility was taken from the courts to the Law Society.

SECTION FOUR

And finally ....

Chapter Twelve

FINAL THOUGHTS

I often sit of an evening thinking back to the Whitstable that I knew from 1920-1939 - a very different town from today. Maybe I am glamorising the old Whitstable but I don't think so for I remember only too well the poverty and the frustration of trying to better myself at work and not being able to do so because of the lack of opportunities.

Some speak of that period as 'the good old days' and others think the opposite but you can't generalise for in every decade there are advantages and disadvantages, depending on your circumstances.

Probably having been away from the town for over fifty years, I can now make comparisons more objectively than if I had remained there. I have been saddened by some things and heartened by others.

As I walk away from the harbour and note the absence of barges and the inactivity along Tankerton beach, it seems so quiet, but I remember the lovely atmosphere. It wasn't noisy but busy with the happy and exhilarating feeling of holiday time, crowds of holidaymakers and the locals strolling along past the bazaars. Where there were tea shops, swinging boats, pleasure boats, photographers, bubbles and, later on, Offredi's tea dances, today there is nothing at all.

In the town, perhaps the little shops didn't make a fortune but they had existed for generations. The small shops in the side streets used their front rooms to carry on their business. Where the alleys were kept neat and the low-fenced gardens, possibly with a chicken run or shed, were the pride and joy of the residents, there are now high fences obscuring the houses.

The sea wall, a necessity, has done nothing to enhance the appearance of beaches such as Reeves' Beach where you could sit on the benches and look out to sea or where the children could run down the sparsely grassed slope to the water. The Horsebridge is now quiet because of the closure of the Oyster Fisheries building and the shipyards. Further along at West Beach, the Red Spider cafe, the Sea Cadets' training ship and the Boating Lake are no longer there.

The Winkle railway line was closed for passenger service and the railway bridge was demolished - an act of sheer vandalism with not even a plaque to tell of its existence. I cannot understand why the railway track was not made into a nature trail which would surely have been an opportunity to bring hikers and ramblers into the town as they have done in other areas. It does not have to become just another resort for within a few miles there are towns that can provide noisy amusements - not everyone wants noise.

On the other side of the coin, a great number of improvements have been made, some of them thanks to the Improvement Trust.

Starvation Point is no longer an eyesore. For instance, the houses along Middle and Island Wall were neglected and run down and now they are well cared for.

Modern flats have been built for the elderly plus a day centre. Another centre, originally in Cromwell Road, is now based in Vulcan Avenue and the Umbrella Club in the Parish Hall.

You can now call in at St Alpheges for a snack.

There is also a much needed museum, an excellent library, a swimming pool, a theatre and, at long last, an addition to the War Memorial in honour of the servicemen who were killed in the last war.

There is not the poverty that we knew, thank goodness.

Tankerton has become a town in its own right and Seasalter, Swalecliffe and Chestfield are developing fast.

I have lived in a number of towns and I, like many others, regard Whitstable as HOME and sincerely hope that future developers and the powers that be respect the remnants of Old Whitstable without holding back progress for it has great potential.

Notes